Transforming Visions
Managing Values in Schools

Dea Alisa

with lots of love and
thanks for your ongoing
friendship through highs
and lows

Pat xx

Transforming Visions
Managing Values in Schools

Dr Ruth Deakin Crick

Middlesex University Press

First published in 2002 by Middlesex University Press

Middlesex University Press is an imprint of
MU Ventures Limited
Bounds Green Road, London N11 2NQ

A CIP catalogue record for this book is available from
The British Library

ISBN 1 898253 47 1

Cover Design by HT Graphics
Photographs courtesy of Dame Alice Owens School and
Aylwood School, Enfield
Typeset by Rekha Khimji

Manufacture coordinated in UK from the Authors CRC
by Book-in-Hand Limited, London N6 5AH

Dedication

Dedicated to Sister Aileen and Nick Wolterstorff whose support and inspiration sustained me.

Acknowledgements

This study could not have taken place without the energy and commitment of teachers, pupils, governors and others. In particular I would like to thank the following teachers and colleagues: Richard Badley, Linda Beskeen, Edward Davies, Nicky Egginton, Steve Evans, Dave Hargreaves, Dorothy Holladay, Claire Macklin, David McGregor, Peter Midgley, Lisa Pascoe and Gary Prosser.

This project has been funded from various sources. Thanks are due to the trustees of the Whitefield Institute, The Temple Ecclesiastical Charity, Oak Hill Trust, The British and Foreign Bible Society and The Teacher Training Agency and to the governors and staff and pupils of St Mary Redcliffe and Temple School, Bristol.

Whole school approaches to spiritual, moral, social and cultural development and citizenship: a case study.

Introduction

Michael Fullan's (Fullan 1993) exploration of educational reforms over the last thirty years has led him to conclude that we have been 'fighting an ultimately fruitless uphill battle'. He argues that rather than designing new reform strategies, innovations or policies what we need is a new mindset, or a fundamental shift of mind, about education. That mindset is one in which managing moral purpose and 'change agentry' is central to productive educational change.

At the heart of teaching is moral purpose – a vision about 'the good life', a focus on ultimate questions of meaning and purpose. Also at the heart of teaching is notion of change, and 'change agentry'. Teachers seek to change the ways pupils think, feel and perceive the world and their place in it.

Understanding and managing those processes of change in a conscious and defensible manner is at the heart of the usual understanding of the reflective practitioner. That is a teacher who is committed to a professional lifestyle in which she or he thinks deeply about their practice, evaluates it and is constantly seeking to improve it. However change, or striving for improvement without an ultimate focus or purpose, becomes simply an end in itself, or it serves unexamined and maybe even unhelpful ends. In his later work Fullan uses the language of spirituality interchangeably with the language of 'moral purpose', a move which links an understanding of spirituality with the ultimate concerns and purposes of schooling.

One of the central debates about values education surrounds the question of whose values should schools be promoting, with concerns about the impact of imposing external values on unsuspecting pupils in the name of education. No school, however, can claim to be value free, or neutral in terms of the worldview, values and ultimate concerns which it will promote through the hidden curriculum and through its own development processes. All schools promote values and worldviews all of the time through the whole experience of schooling. To be ethical and professional in schooling, especially in a diverse society where there is no longer consensus in a universalising belief system, it is critical that schools are able to be explicit and articulate about their values, beliefs and purposes. There is an intimate relationship between a school's vision and values (both lived and espoused) and the spiritual, moral, social and cultural development of pupils in that school – both actual and desired. What a school considers to be the most important in terms of achievement and direction, and those goals and targets, imposed or chosen, which shape practice and define what is possible, will significantly shape the emerging value systems of the pupils living within that system.

Across western democracies similar themes have emerged in education policies over the last twenty years –self management of schools, improving pupils' learning outcomes through measurable standards, diversity, parental and community involvement. Alongside this there has been increasing concern about morality and values, with major initiatives in these areas such as the character education movement in the USA, and the citizenship and values agenda in the UK.

So much professional development in education focuses on strategic processes, measurable outcomes and the technology of managing schools as learning institutions. There is far less material that deals with the 'softer' side of schools, or less easily measurable things, such as quality of relationships, or spiritual and moral development. In fact very often these two sides of schools, like Barber's (Barber 1996) twin education crises, are seen as unrelated to each other. It is the contention of this book that the two sides of schooling are equally important and that the 'softer' side of values and spirituality can be managed, measured, improved upon and used as a defensible alternative 'voice' in the cacophony of the competing demands and pressures of contemporary school leadership.

This book explores the ideas and practice of 'values' in education and schooling, and draws significantly upon a particular case-study. This case study took place in a Voluntary Aided comprehensive school in a large city, where a team of teachers developed policy and practice in the area of spiritual, moral, social and cultural development of pupils and citizenship over a period of four years. The project began with a critical exploration of QCA draft guidance, and developed into a whole scale approach to values education which incorporates the citizenship requirements. As with any case study, it is not generalisable, but there are ideas, processes and practices emerging from it which may encourage understanding and stimulate further development and practice. A team of between four and eight teachers, including the head and a deputy worked on different aspects of the project over a four-year period. They were facilitated by an external researcher who worked with the teachers in school, developing strategies for school based research and development work. The project was funded from various local sources, and included a Teacher Training Agency Project Grant during its third year.

Transforming Visions
Managing Values in Schools

Chapter One
Exploring Vision and Values

Vision as the story we live by

In 'The End of Education' Postman argues that education that has lost its story, or its purpose, is dead (Postman 1996). He uses the term 'narrative' or 'god' to describe the concept of 'story' or 'purpose' in education and talks of the gods (or stories) of economism, utility and technicism which are served by contemporary education systems world-wide. These gods or narratives offer a means of making sense of the world, and one's place in it. They offer a rationale for the way things are and a hope for the future. Take for example the narrative or god of economism – described by Postman as a 'cold, hard god', offering the reward of a good job for those who work hard. The other two gods of the contemporary trinity he describes as the god of consumership which offers the promise of an increasing array of consumer goods as a means of achieving happiness, and the god of technology, which offers the possibility of answers to all of life's questions including death itself!

The need for a purpose or a reason for life and for education is a primary human need. Individuals and communities need a hope, a planned for future and something to live for. In the same way a school without a purpose or a vision lacks direction and focus. Whilst schools are inundated with performance targets, for pupils and staff, and targets arising from OFSTED inspections, targets alone do not constitute a vision. A vision has more depths, more hope and more meaning than simply measurable targets.

Teachers, by and large, have vision. They are generally very moral people who care a lot about children and society and about their own teaching subject. Teaching attracts people like this, although all too often teachers' sense of vision and energy for teaching is swamped by day to day demands and pressures of change. The discourse of education has become littered with the language of managerialism – SMART targets, school development plans, line managers, performance management and so on, but it is not so rich in the language of vision and hope, or values or virtue.

It is informative to read documentation from government agencies about education with questions of vision in mind:

- Who is being served?
- To what end?
- What is of ultimate concern?

Inevitably, that which is considered to be the most important, will squeeze out that which is considered to be less important. No school is value free. Education progressively nurtures children into a particular worldview, with its associated 'ultimate concerns' and spirituality – even if that spirituality is something like Hull's (Hull 1996) description of the 'spirituality of capitalism'. The question is not whether this will happen, but how.

There is therefore an intimate relationship between a school's vision and values (both lived and espoused) and the spiritual, moral, social and cultural development of pupils in that school – both actual and desired. What a school considers to be the most important in terms of achievement and direction, and those goals and targets, imposed or chosen, which shape practice and define what is possible, will significantly shape the emerging value systems of the pupils living within that system.

Vision is drawn from ideas about what matters for young people and the future of society. Leadership requires vision as well as the skills and resources to implement it. Fullan argues that we need the fusion of ideas, with moral purpose or spirituality, and with the power to deliver if we are to harness the forces of change in schooling and engage in educational reform.

'Ideas without moral purpose are a dime a dozen. Moral purpose without ideas means being all dressed up with nowhere to go. Power without ideas and moral purpose is deadly. Moral purpose and ideas without power means the train never leaves the station.'(Fullan 1999)

> *Everyone who works in a school is entitled to a unique personal vision of the way he or she would like the school to become, but has an obligation to uncover, discover, and rediscover what the vision is and contribute to it to the betterment of the school community.'* (Barth 1990)

The School's Vision as a Foundation for a Whole School Approach

The starting point for any whole school approach to citizenship education, or spiritual, moral, social and cultural development of pupils is the vision and the core values of the school. These can inform and shape a whole school approach that is coherent across subjects and across classrooms. One of the pathologies of the information age, and often of the National Curriculum, is the packaging up of knowledge into discreet subjects that do not appear to the learner to relate to each other. Making sense of large amounts of information, selecting what is important, leaving what is not important and integrating bits of knowledge into a developing worldview framework is an increasing critical task for today' learners. A school with a robust vision which is located within a community and tradition/s and which is explicit about what is considered to be of ultimate importance has a means of providing a curriculum coherence which does not come packaged in the National Curriculum. This does not mean the school has to have a religious foundation – but it does mean that the school needs to be clear and explicit about its ultimate concerns, and the belief systems and cultural traditions which it draws upon for that vision.

A second reason why the school community's own vision is foundational for any whole school approach to this area is that it is simply that – the vision owned by the school community of which the learners are a part. To be able to say to pupils in the processes of teaching and learning, that 'these values are what we, in our community (including you), hold to be most important', is a powerful learning tool. It engages the learner in a different way from simply the presentation of an abstract problem, or an isolated task. It invites the pupil as a participating citizen, or member of a community, to engage with their learning, to develop healthy critical thinking, to make value judgements, and to clarify their own beliefs and attitudes. In other words it helps to bring the real world into the classroom and to relate learning to the real world.

A third reason why the school's own vision and values are a critical starting point for a whole school approach is that once a community has determined what it holds to be of ultimate concern, or ultimate value, then that community has a means of becoming more self-determined in its practice. It can be critical of wider value systems that are present in society. The problem of imposing external values, from external religious or political sources of authority, becomes far less significant, because the community itself becomes the final arbiter about what it ultimately values. It will inevitably draw upon those external political, cultural and religious traditions which form the wider context of life in contemporary society, since it is impossible to separate out the factors which form individual and communal worldviews and belief systems. However a school community's owned vision also becomes a local 'third voice' with which to contribute to the debate and to decision-making processes.

Links between vision and values and the spiritual, moral, social and cultural dimensions of education?

The spiritual dimension of education is one that is considered to be problematic by many headteachers, and there is by no means unanimous agreement about the meaning of the term. In a study of headteachers' views from three Local Authorities in Wales in 1996, 24.8% were uncertain about, or in disagreement with the statement that schools should have a responsibility for spiritual development. (Davies G.1996)

Often spirituality is understood as something related only to Religious Education and Worship and notions of God. It is designated as part of a person's individual private life, and therefore largely irrelevant to the central task of schooling. In the same way 'values' are often seen as an 'add on' to schooling - things we believe in and must promote - but separate from and uninfluenced by the delivery of the curriculum. If spirituality is a capability of all human beings and has to do with our vision of life and our ultimate concerns, then it is possible and desirable in our contemporary, diverse society to develop a more robust and educationally defensible understanding and practice of spirituality.

Wright's (Wright 1998) definition of spirituality is one that is particularly helpful:

> *'Spirituality is the developing relationship of the individual, within community and tradition, to that which is - or is perceived to be - of ultimate concern, ultimate value and ultimate truth'. Page 88.*

Schools will inevitably transmit their ultimate concerns and values - what for that community is ultimately true and of value. Thus the more coherent and thoughtful a school can be in its understanding of its ultimate aims and purposes, the more effectively it will deliver the spiritual, moral, social and cultural development of pupils and all aspects of preparation for adult life. This is intimately related to the school community's vision and values.

On the basis of these ideas, the spiritual component of spiritual, moral, social and cultural development can be seen to be generative or foundational for the moral, social and cultural components. The following table expresses this:

Table 1 Definitions of SMSC

	Definitions
Spiritual	Signifies what we/I believe about the meaning and purpose of life. A community's ultimate concerns and values.
Moral	Because of what we believe about the meaning and purpose of life we live by principles and codes which guide our choices between right and wrong.
Social	Our way of relating to self and others which is influenced by our spirituality and morality.
Cultural	The ways in which we do things – the rites, rituals, customs and practices which develop over time within communities. Culture gives specific expression to a community's spirituality, morality, and social values.

(Deakin Crick et al 2000)

From vision to mission

School leaders' deepest educational beliefs and values are important sources of communal energy and should specifically inform their school's vision and mission statement. Headteachers, are of course, leaders but there are many more partners in schools who lead, and vision always needs to be negotiated and shared. The terms vision statement and mission statement are often used interchangeably and this can cause confusion. In broad terms a vision statement is more general and overarching than a mission statement, which is specific, localised and forms a concrete foundation for school planning. A mission statement draws upon, and localises a vision for education.

A mission statement should:

- Be visionary
- Clarify the main intentions and purposes of the organisation
- Describe the school's main activities
- State the school's key values
- Be backed by the intention and capability to live up to it.
- Be a starting point for development plans and staff development and appraisal

Values or virtues inherent in the vision and mission

A school's mission statement will have embedded within it some core principles or values which provide a guiding framework for the actual implementation of the vision and mission. The term 'values' is widely used in educational literature and policymaking, and at heart refers to something that has 'worth'. However in schooling, and in this case study, the term is used more specifically to refer to particular ethical values or principles.

Definition

A core value is a guiding spiritual and moral or ethical principle by which a community seeks to live. Core values arise out of what we believe to be important about people, about society and about learning and knowledge. A core value represents a 'good' in itself. Core values are inherent in a communal belief system, or ideology, as a core cluster of beliefs and attitudes that point towards the 'good life'. The extent to which individuals share belief and value systems determines the extent to which a community can be said to own shared values. Core values are 'lived' as well as espoused, and living in a way that is consistent with core values within a community is intrinsically a part of the desired 'good life'.

Core values and spiritual, moral, social and cultural development

The case study research began with an attempt to develop a whole school approach to spiritual, moral, social and cultural development of pupils. Along with the OFSTED inspection framework and the draft guidance offered by the Qualifications and Curriculum Authority the research team began with the assumption that spiritual development would be treated separately from moral development, which would be separate from social and cultural development. Apart from the excessive amount of work this required, it was extremely difficult to separate out the experience of spiritual development from moral and social development and so on. Rather the team observed that when a pupil was engaging with questions of values and ethics within the curriculum then it was possible for all of those types of development to be taking place in the same learning process. To separate them out was felt to be artificial and unrealistic in terms of how human beings experience the world. Thus the idea of the school's core values as 'carriers' of, or vehicles for, the spiritual, moral, social and cultural development of pupils began to emerge amongst the research team. Core ethical values were seen to have spiritual, moral, social and cultural components to them, and were understood as desirable ends in themselves, a focus for vision, something that can be aspired towards, which can shape the direction of a community or a society.

For example, justice is numbered among the values identified by the National Forum for Values in Education and the Community. It is also a core value that many school communities would espouse as important. Pupils are likely to use the language of 'fairness' and many teachers are more familiar with the term 'equality'. Whilst an exact and dogmatic agreement about the definition of the idea of justice would be impossible, and was not attempted in the case study school, the idea was something that mattered a lot to the school community. Young people and children have a strong sense of what is fair and unfair, as do many adults. Their commitment to the idea is an emotional and intellectual one, and where the idea shapes the manner in which they live, and their hopes and aspirations, then it can also be seen as a spiritual and moral commitment.

The example of justice

Justice has a distinctly spiritual component to it. A belief in justice as something that has purpose and meaning, which human beings feel passionately about, indicates the nature of its spirituality. Differing communities with differing worldviews and belief systems understand the nature of justice differently – a Christian spirituality of justice is different in content to Bhuddist spirituality of justice, which is different again to the ultimate concerns of justice for a humanist, but nevertheless justice is an idea, or a guiding principle which has the power to motivate and inspire human activity. When a pupil is challenged in her learning by the injustices of the slave trade, for example, and is emotionally and intellectually engaged with that learning, it is highly likely that spiritual development is taking place. The pupil is examining the idea, making her own judgements about it, reflecting upon it and possibly internalising her own version of justice, moving towards her own commitment and action.

However justice also has a moral component, to do with how society is structured so that each person and group has the freedom and opportunity to develop as a full human being. Pupils care about being fair and being treated fairly, and the implications for social development are self-evident. Doing justice is something that happens within a specific location and culture – and the manner in which justice is pursued and practised may differ according to the cultural situation, whether locally in a community or nationally on a global stage.

Academically, of course, the term justice is debated widely with differing views about what constitutes justice in any given situation. What is empirically obvious is that justice or fairness does matter to young people – even those of primary school age have strong feelings and views about fairness, or the lack of fairness. It is the space between these two extremes that is the terrain of spiritual and moral development in schools.

In schools lengthy and exact academic definitions are difficult, if not impossible, to achieve, and even if this was achieved one might wonder what practical use it would be.   What does matter, however, is the quality of discourse about justice and fairness within the school community.   All healthy communities have codes of ethical values by which to live. There are core values or virtues about which our society has some agreement but each school and community is likely to be distinctive in its emphasis and approach.

Being explicit is important

The notion of a school, or a community, being value-free is no longer tenable, nor is the separation of 'facts from values', or the notion that some aspects of school life, say numeracy and literacy strategies, are somehow value-neutral.   Value judgements are made implicitly and explicitly through what is taught or not taught, throughout the whole of the school development planning process, including the context of the school, its external relationships, the leadership and management policies and practices, the teaching and learning strategies and the content of the curriculum. No aspect of school community life is exempt from making a contribution to the 'lived' values of the school and therefore to the spiritual, moral, social and cultural formation of pupils within its community.

Thus even if a school is not explicit about its vision and its core values it will be living and promoting beliefs and core values of some kind. These may be ones of which the school might be deeply critical and which may run counter to its stated aims. At the very least, a lack of explicitness makes it harder to have any notion of shared vision and values.

Difference, discrepancies and dialogue

However, the identification of a shared vision and values does not mean that conflict or debate will be eradicated, nor even that this would be desirable. In fact, a healthy school will be one that can handle conflict and debate and see that as something that healthy communities need to do, and which can be held respectfully within a commitment to dialogue, and to growth. Coping with difference, learning to respect alternatives, identifying discrepancies between action and aspiration and being critical of society in the light of a particular vision is an essential part of healthy spiritual, moral, social and cultural development for all learners. Where a community or society can no longer embrace and respond to criticism and change from within then that society or community becomes static, totalitarian and less likely to grow, develop and expand.

Chapter Two
Case Study: Clarifying the school's vision and values.

Introduction

In the years before the values project began the school had undertaken a lot of work involving teachers and governors in reformulating the vision and mission of the school, prior to the appointment of the headteacher. The school development plan was in place in detail and included a focus on improving spiritual development within the school. This earlier work was developed in the values project through a process of consultation that identified some shared core moral and spiritual values that emerged from the school's vision statement.

As well as identifying what the school community said was important, the researchers also wanted to know what the pupils, teachers and parents and governors actually valued in practice. Was the 'talk' backed up by action? This led to the second strand of initial research, which was to investigate the 'lived' values and attitudes of a sample of pupils and staff in the school (described in the following chapter).

Consultation Phase

Given the working definition of values agreed by the research team, a process of consultation was initiated with a significant majority of members of the school community. This included pupils, parents, governors and teachers and the purpose was to be able to identify a set of core values which the school community could be said to agree upon as being important enough to guide the conduct and direction of the school.

Use was made of materials, then in development by the Institute for Global Ethics (Born P, Paula M, Mulligan J. & Price E 2002) for defining shared values within a community.

Essentially part of this programme entails working with a group of students to define the term 'values', in particular 'moral values', and then to go through a process of group decision making which results in a set of values which represent the consensus set of that particular group. This process is not dissimilar to those developed within the Total Quality Management movement (Marsh 1993).

The consultation was piloted by a teacher member of the research team and a group of 'A' level sociology students who embarked upon a consultation of the whole of the sixth form. The findings of this pilot were that, even amongst sixth-formers, the language of values was one that was not readily entered into by contemporary pupils, or their teachers, and there needed to be some explanation of terms and experimentation with language. For example the difference between values and moral values was not easily understood - some pupils valued 'good looks', and others recommended values which are actually character dispositions, which could lead to both desirable and undesirable ends. 'Hardworking', for instance, is an attribute that could equally apply to Adolf Hitler and Mother Theresa, and therefore was not valid as a moral 'end' in itself, whereas 'caring' is more likely to be considered as a desirable end in itself for the whole community. The lack of familiarity with the language of moral and spiritual values was a significant point – without a language with which to name experience, hope and vision it is difficult to move beyond vague ideals and the 'woolly language' of awe and wonder.

Pupils Teachers and Parents Consultation

The consultation process was extended to all pupils and teachers, through four subject departments, which, between them provided lesson time for all classes in the school, apart from year eleven (16 year olds) who had 'mock' examinations. Thus all pupils, except year eleven, and their teachers participated in the consultation. The student researchers then provided a structure for the consultation, including guidelines for the teachers. Each consultation was observed by a student researcher, who recorded the set of between five and seven values that the pupil group decided upon. The Parent Teacher Association devoted a session to this process, at an open meeting for parents and a significant proportion of pupils were given a questionnaire to discuss with their parents following their own consultation in school.

Governors: Specific Tasks

The governing body consultation took place in a similar manner, although for the governors the task was twofold. Firstly to identify values which represented a consensus and secondly to identify values, ideally the same set, which could be defensibly argued to be intrinsic to the Christian tradition. This latter task is a particular responsibility of Foundation Governors in Voluntary Aided schools, whose duty is to ensure that the school remains true to the aims of its Trust Deed. In this case, the Trust Deed required that

> 'the foundation governors shall hold the trust property upon trust to permit the same to be used for the purposes of the School which shall be in union with and conducted upon the principles and in furtherance of the ends and designs of the National Society'.

The National Society is the education arm of the Church of England, therefore the foundation governors had a specific duty to ensure that the school's vision and values was in keeping with the teachings of the Church of England and more specifically that the school should be conducted in a manner in which the practice of education is shaped by the beliefs and values of the Judeo-Christian tradition.

Findings: Values Consultation - Pupils and Teachers

The values identified by the groups of pupils with their teachers were collated and examined by the research team. Where differing words were used to name similar values, then the values were clustered into groups. For example there were several values named which related to friendship and kindness, or more generally, positive interpersonal relationships. These were clustered into one group under the heading friendship and kindness, which was the most popular term.

Altogether 30 teaching groups and their teachers were consulted producing 206 votes, though only 11 of those votes were recorded from teachers. There were a number of votes that were not included because they represented character dispositions rather than core values. Whilst every effort was made to be accurate in the detailed representation of this data, it is impossible to be absolutely specific because of the nature of the work, the number of participant pupil researchers and the time-scale. However it was possible to be confident in the overall results and the relative importance of differing values to the school population at that point in time.

There were certain values that occurred with remarkable consistency across all groups consulted, although the language employed to describe them often varied. If, as Kelly (1995) suggests, a construct or a value can be described as a discrimination, or as part of the way one stands towards one's world as a complete person, then the use of different words to describe the same or similar values can be justified.

The overall results are presented in table two below. A more detailed analysis can be found in Appendix A

Table 2

Value Cluster	Number of group votes
Friendship and Kindness	62
Honesty, Truth and Integrity	31
Trust, Loyalty, Trustworthiness	38
Respect for self, others environment	30
Fairness	23
Forgiveness	9
Faith	4
Education, growth, development	9

Parents

The list of core values recommended by parents attending a meeting of the Parent Teacher Association (PTA) was as follows:

Table 3

PTA recommended values	alternative responses/additions
Care and Compassion	understanding,
Honesty	reliability, integrity.
Respect for others	
Respect for the environment	
Justice/Fairness	tolerance,
Self Esteem	pride in self, responsibility for self,
	Christian values/God's values
	Trustworthiness, loyalty

Following the pupil consultation, pupils were given a homework task to discuss the values consultation with their parent/s and to request their response to the values proposed by the PTA. This elicited 38 written responses from parents, which broadly endorsed the original set, sometimes using different terminology to represent similar ideas. In addition there were recommendations to include excellence, trustworthiness and to include reference to the tradition of Christianity as the source of the school's values.

Governors

The set of values which the governors identified as desirable for the school community to work with and as intrinsic to the Christian faith were as follows:

Table 4

Core Value	Alternative wording
The intrinsic value of the human person - self and others 'love your neighbour as yourself'	consideration, kindness respect
Human Rights and Justice Global and Local	fairness, tolerance
Reconciliation and Forgiveness	suffering with
Truth	honesty, reliability
Caring for the Environment Global and Local	stewardship
Fulfilling our potential	striving for excellence, perfection
Faith in Christ	spirituality

Consensus Values or Values intrinsic in an external tradition?

One of the central debates generated by this consultation work was that surrounding the tension arising from the question of whose values should the school be promoting. Berkovitz suggests that with reference to the content of moral education there are three broad approaches that appear incompatible. These are the indoctrinative (traditional) approach which identifies a specific, and externally validated set of values or virtues; the Romanticist approach which avoids identifying moral content at all since content is idiosyncratic and latent in the individual; and the Cognitive-Structural (constructivist) approach in which content is viewed as a pedagogical tool - a means to an end.

Clearly a consensus set of values, which are meaningful to the pupil population will be most consistent with the cognitive-structural approach and with liberal theory. In a context of postmodernity and the presence in contemporary society of multiple belief systems and worldviews it is difficult to sustain a logical argument for a universal belief system which can provide a foundation for education. Thus the attraction of the consensus approach with its inherently relativist account is evident - we might ask whose 'bag of virtues' shall we choose? The answer is 'our own bag'.

However a difficulty with a purely relativist approach, is that not advocating a specific content is covertly endorsing an ethical position that there is no absolute right or wrong, and that truth or goodness is ultimately unknowable. This, of course, when promoted as the right approach, is internally inconsistent.

On a practical level it was evident in this consultation that there was a considerable degree of consensus in those values which are important to the school community. This finding is not new - indeed the SCAA consultation discovered the same, as did the Josephson Institute's 1992 Youth Summit Conference in the USA which generated the 'six pillars of character' (Trustworthiness, Respect, Responsibility, Fairness, Caring and Citizenship) which are included in federal legislation.

This degree of consensus is interesting, suggesting that there are perhaps some core values or principles which lead to healthy human community which are common to all humanity (Kidder 1997). However it is possible that a consensus-only approach might lead to values such as white supremacy, racism or elitism. Less dramatically there could be deep division in a school community, for example, about issues surrounding meritocracy and elitism in terms of ability. Berkovitiz (ibid) argues that if one is to be truly moral about moral education, there must be some form of justification for content that transcends local tastes.

In addition the consensus approach avoids the question of the belief system or worldview from which the values are derived. The implicit assumption is that where there is a consensus on values, then those values are derived from the same belief system, or worldview. If our values are part of our belief systems, then that belief system or underlying worldview is also an important part of the equation. In contemporary society there are a number of belief systems present and embodied in differing communities. The task of justification of the consensus values becomes more complex where there are multiple communities of belief present in a school community.

In this case the school is a Voluntary Aided Church of England school whose foundation governors are required by their Trust Deed to ensure that the school's aims and purposes are shaped by and consistent with the principles and practice of the Church of England. Thus a Christian world and life view, with its truth claims, is required by law to shape the aims and values of the school.

The list of values promoted by the governing body included two values which did not appear widely in the consultation namely 'faith in Christ' and 'love of learning'. The value of learning could be argued to be a central component of a school community whose central task is teaching and learning. 'Faith in Christ' is argued to be central to a Christian world and life view. Thus these two values, which are derived from tradition rather than significant consensus, were felt by the governors to be essential components of the school's espoused values.

Core Values Defined

In the light of these debates the research team compiled a list of values which could be offered to the school community as a list which represents both consensus and engagement with the tradition of Christianity. Each value is an umbrella label for a cluster of related values, and it was noted that language use needs to be appropriate to the particular audience. This list comprises:

- Valuing ourselves
- Valuing others
- Justice
- Forgiveness
- Truth
- Trustworthiness
- Stewardship
- Fulfilling our potential
- Faith in Christ

Chapter Three
Case Study: Investigating Current Practice

1. Introduction

This strand of the research was designed to investigate those values that operate in practice - through the perceptions of pupils and teachers. The research team decided to use a research instrument known as repertory grid technique - developed by Kelly (1955) within the framework of personal construct theory. It is a form of structured interview that gives some indication as to the subject's core constructs in relation to school. According to Horley (1991) the terms 'values' and 'constructs' can be used interchangeably. Thus this technique will give valuable insights as to the sorts of values which are important in practice to a sample of members of the school community.

2. Samples of the Population

The student researchers used the repertory grid technique with 30 pupils. The pupils were selected to form a representative sample of the population. The sample took into account age, ability, race and gender. The sample represented approximately 2.7% of the population.

The research team used the repertory grid technique with 8 teachers and two members of the support staff, which represented approximately 20% of the population. The teachers were selected to represent a range of experience, roles and a balance of gender.

3. Personal Construct Theory and Repertory Grid technique

The repertory grid technique is a research tool initiated by Kelly (1955) to support research within the framework of personal construct psychology. Kelly worked as a teacher and as a counsellor and his theory grew out of his need to understand, predict and have an effect upon his clients and his students. One of his major contributions was to insist that the need to understand, predict and have an effect upon was not simply a need of scientists, but is a fundamental attribute of the way persons exist in the world. Understanding the other person was to Kelly achievable only in so far as one can know how that person goes about making sense of his or her world. Each individual has a personal construct system, which is a developed set of representations or models of the world. Some of this is developed through social experience, some of it is pre-verbal and some of it is verbally transmitted although not all of it is readily accessible to the individual in terms of self-consciously held concepts. For all individuals this construct system is to some degree shared with others and to some degree unique to the individual.

Unlike other psychological theories Kelly presented personal construct psychology as a complete and formal statement of a theory. It is a reflexive theory that attempts to redefine psychology as a psychology of persons, rather than reducing psychology to a static, biological or analytical model. He is not proposing personal construct theory as a contradiction of the other psychologies but as an alternative to them. It does not deny the 'truths' of other theories but may provide more interesting, inspiring and useful ways of using those 'truths'. In this sense it is a useful tool for this research, with its view of the person as a whole, active learner about the world, whose understanding is constituted in the constructs with which the person makes meaning out of his or her experience.

The theory of personal constructs is formally stated as a fundamental postulate and eleven corollaries. The fundamental postulate is that a person's processes are psychologically channelised by the ways in which they anticipate events. This striving for personal meaning leads to the following corollaries:

- Construction corollary: a person anticipates events by construing their replications.

- Individuality corollary: persons differ from each other in their construction of events.
- Organisation Corollary: each person characteristically evolves, for their convenience in anticipating events, a construction system embracing ordinal relationships between constructs.
- Dichotomy corollary: a person's construction system is composed of a finite number of dichotomous constructs.
- Choice corollary: persons choose for themselves that alternative in a dichotomised construct through which they anticipate the greater possibility for the elaboration of their system.
- Experience Corollary: a person's construction system varies as they successively construe the replication of events.
- Modulation Corollary: the variation in a person's construction system is limited by the permeability of the constructs within whose range of convenience the variants lie.
- Fragmentation Corollary: a person may successively employ a variety of construction subsystems which are inferentially incompatible with each other.
- Commonality Corollary: to the extent that one person employs a construction of experience which is similar to that employed by another, their processes are psychologically similar to those of the other person.
- Sociality Corollary: to the extent that one person construes the construction processes of another they may play a role in a social process involving the other person.

One of the criticisms of personal construct psychology is that it is purely a description of thinking and thus only deals with one aspect of the person. However Kelly did not accept this dualist approach to cognition and emotion which he sees as a descendant of ancient dualisms between reason and passion, mind and body and thinking and feeling. Personal construct psychology is an attempt to talk about people in a unitary language, and the constructs are not simply words just because the theory itself is systematic, articulate and rational. He defines a construct, not as a thought or a feeling but as a discrimination, it is part of the way one stands towards one's world as a complete person.

This theoretical framework which underlies the repertory grid technique is evidently compatible with an interactionist view of social relations and the social construction of reality, and the anthropological understanding of values, attitudes and beliefs which underpins this research project. It provides a useful way of understanding how individuals within the school construe their role, their task and their context.

4. Repertory Grid - a Research Instrument

Fransella and Bannister suggest that the repertory grid 'is perhaps best looked on as a particular form of structured interview' (1977 p4) which formalises the process of understanding how the other person views their world, what connections there are within their framework and what is important or unimportant - in other words their values. The grid assigns mathematical values to the relationships between a person's constructs and enables the researcher to focus on particular subsystems of construing. It enables us to understand what is unique and surprising about the structure and content of a person's outlook on the world, and is really a formalised version of the kind of information which human beings are always in the process of eliciting from each other.

The repertory grid was chosen as an instrument for this research because it offered a formalised and structured means of eliciting the working world views of the pupils and teachers in school. It offers a thorough and defensible interpretation of the teaching and learning world as these subjects see it, and it is less distortable by researcher bias or 'edubabble' where the subject says what they think the education researcher wants to hear, based on the circulating official discourses, or on the pupil's desire to please and 'get it right'. Thus the technique has a lot to offer to this project which is seeking to explore the links between espoused values of the school and the actual values in practice.

The repertory grid is essentially a grid whose vertical axis comprises elements which represent the area in which construing is to be investigated and whose horizontal axis represents the differing ways in which the subject construes those elements.

Elements

In this case the elements represented differing aspects of the school. A decision was taken to supply elements to the subjects because this would give a degree of consistency to the results. In other words the domain in which construing was to be investigated would be the same for both the pupils and the teachers in the study. The elements were identified through a semi-structured interview with the headteacher and the two deputy heads, who were asked to imagine they were showing the researcher around their school. They were asked then to identify anything of importance to them which they would like to draw attention to. The researchers stressed that they were colleagues engaged in research, rather than a prospective parent or inspector. This produced three lists of practical aspects of school life. The three lists were examined to identify those elements which were common to all three and one list was compiled which included elements from all three lists.

Using three members of the school leadership team ensured that those elements supplied were ones which were significant to the school leaders and therefore to the direction of the school in terms of development planning. It can be argued that the elements supplied to the subjects were symbolic of the vision of the school, thus providing a useful focus for the research, and indeed for the school itself in terms of evaluation and development. However a weakness of this method was that it could leave out elements of the school which are actually important to the pupils or teachers but which do not feature highly in the articulated vision of the school. An example of this is that early on it became clear to researchers that, for pupils, 'friends' were an important element of school life which did not appear on the supplied list. Interestingly, however, the importance of interpersonal relationships appeared strongly in the pupils' construing, suggesting that this did not necessarily invalidate the data.

Bannister and Fransella (1977) claim that there is no such thing as an element which is only an element or a construct which is nothing but a construct.

Constructs

Kelly (1955) originally described six ways in which the researcher can elicit the constructs in relation to the elements. These were formal methods of using triads, dyads or groups of elements to discover like and unlike, thus eliciting a construct and its contrast pole. In this research project each subject was asked to group the elements in any way that they chose. The researcher and subject then discussed ways in which the elements in the differing groups were the same, and identified the subject's way of construing those elements. The subject was then asked what the opposite of that construct was, which was an approach used by Epting (1971).

The reasons for eliciting, rather than supplying, constructs were that the purpose of the research was to understand the actual meanings and the real teaching and learning world view of the subjects which may not have been represented by a set of constructs which the researcher could supply. Each subject would have no reason to withhold an important construct as may be the case in a clinical setting, and in the case of the teachers, had a high level of understanding about the area under investigation. It was not intended to compare sets of constructs across the sample in detail, although similarities and differences between different subjects was of interest. Also the opportunity to clarify with the subject the precise description of their construct led to much greater idiosyncratic understanding of each individual world view.

Because the repertory grid looks at constructs and not concepts it is able to look at the relationship between constructs, which are bipolar in nature, and therefore to understand the meanings which the subject is working with. The range of convenience of the constructs refer to the finite number of elements to which a given construct and its emerging pole can be applied. Even though the elements were supplied to the subjects there was not a problem with the range of convenience, although in the rating procedure some constructs were identified as 'not particularly related to' certain elements. This indicates that the vision of the school leaders has meaning to both the teachers and pupils in the study, although that meaning may differ between individuals.

Rating of Constructs

The second stage of the creation of the repertory grids was for the subject to rate the constructs against the elements according to their perceived level of association. This stage was only used with the teachers, and not the pupils, for reasons of time and the expertise of the student research team. The rating scale was from one to seven with seven meaning that the construct was highly associated, in the subject's schema with the particular element, and a one meant that the opposite pole of the construct was highly associated with the element. The mid point, number four, was interpreted as 'not particularly associated with' the element.

This then provided the raw data for analysis. The instrument was extremely useful for the research without the rating technique and the subsequent analysis because it provided a means of eliciting a set of values, or working constructs together with their contrast poles which was rooted in practice, rather than risking being a more superficial personal description of the individual's approach to schooling.

However using the rating technique for the teachers' grids enabled some more sophisticated interpretations to be made from the data which was useful. Rating itself, as opposed to rank ordering the constructs or a binary analysis, allowed more flexibility of response and therefore a more precise analysis. By using a correlation statistic (Pearson product-moment) it was possible to make some judgement about the relative importance of one construct compared with another, and one element compared with another. This was done using the GAB programme (Grid Analysis for Beginners) developed by Bannister and Higginbotham which offers a minimal statistical interpretation of raw data. In their manual, Bannister and Higginbotham argue that the popularity of computer packages for analysing grids has threatened to make the grid method itself curiously arthritic and they recommend that the research questions themselves dictate the mode of analysis. In this case, an interpretation of the relative importance of constructs, which means a high level of correlation with other constructs, is useful information since it suggests the dominant mode of thinking/action by the subject. The correlation between the constructs also indicates the level of coherence within a subjects framework.

The Researcher / Subject Relationship

One of the issues, which recurred during the repertory grid interviews, was the nature of the relationship between the researcher and the subject. The elicitation of constructs required researcher skill, and interpretation and therefore potential researcher bias. With a range of researchers there was also the issue of difference in skill and background ideas. To counter this both the student researchers, and the research team undertook a pilot of the repertory grid technique on each other and discussed a format, technique and some precise wording of questions and explanations.

Often the subjects were searching for words to describe their constructs, and the skills of listening, empathy, unconditional positive regard and authenticity were critical in agreeing the wording for a construct that most represented the subjects' form of discrimination. The potential bias was moderated by a careful repetition of the construct with the subject, and a request to confirm that that really did adequately describe what the subject was seeking to elucidate.

5. Findings: Personal Constructs -Teachers and Pupils

The Repertory Grid interviews with 30 pupils, 8 teachers and 2 members of the support staff, were completed by the end of the Autumn term. The interviews with the pupils were undertaken by sociology students in controlled conditions, and simply entailed eliciting a set of personal constructs related to the twenty eight elements of school life which were of importance to the senior management team. The sets of constructs therefore do not define the pupil's entire construct system in relation to school but they represent the ways in which the pupils construe what is important to the school itself.

The personal constructs elicited from the teachers and staff were rated against the elements. The use of a correlation statistic enabled some judgement to be made about which construct was most significant, or most used, in relation to the elements.

The constructs are tabled in Appendix D (teachers and staff) and Appendix E (pupils). The results of the correlations statistic are set out in Appendix F.

Pupils: Valuing Relationships

The thirty pupils, ranging from year seven to year thirteen, provided a total of 286 constructs. Of these 35 (12.2%) appeared to be related to positive interpersonal relationships, particularly friends or peers and teachers. This is of particular interest because the sociology students would have liked to have altered one of the elements to include 'friends', which they all considered to be an important element of school life.

In fact this was evident in the manner in which the pupil sample construed the elements as they were.

In terms of what pupils actually value, it would appear that positive interpersonal relationships are of particular significance. From this data it is difficult to quantify the relative importance of friends, teachers or parents, but the findings of the personal constructs do support the findings of the values consultation, where values relating to friendship and kindness were significantly more important to pupils than any others.

Given that this is the case there are implications for policies on spiritual, moral, social and cultural development which need to be taken into account. Firstly interpersonal relationships are primarily experiential and biographical and difficult to quantify in terms of quality. Whilst there are important aspects of relationships which can be known and understood cognitively essentially relationships engage the whole person and are not dependent upon being understood intellectually. Recent research on moral development and the development of autonomy has stressed the importance of recognising the social and historical context in which education takes place, and in particular the importance of relationships and language in that context (Wertsch 1989, Witheral & Pope Edwards 1991, Shweder 1982, Sampson 1989 Tappan 1991). Whilst not abandoning the importance of rationality, in particular the role of critical reflection in education, greater credence is now being given to the role of affect, imagination and anthropological considerations. Gilligan (1982) and Noddings (1984) favour an alternative conception to the 'autonomous self' as a conception of 'persons in relation' and Shweder and Sampson talk of the persons as 'socially constituted beings' (ibid).

Not only do pupils appear to be significantly aware of the importance of relationships but also relationships appear to constitute the context in which spiritual, moral, social and cultural development takes place. To the extent that relationships contribute to the culture of the school then this also becomes an important component for consideration.

Relationships are experienced and modelled rather than taught at the blackboard. However the related disciplines of psychology and of psychotherapy indicate that there is also a great deal that is known about interpersonal relationships, and concepts of the self, and that that information and understanding can significantly enhance relationships and social behaviour. Clearly there are implications here for the content of Personal and Social Education in schools, where such understanding and information might be systematically promoted.

Valuing the Self

Constructs relating to self identity were also significantly present amongst the pupils. 29 (10.1%) related to individual expression, personal freedom, standing up for oneself or following new ideas. Overlapping with this were constructs relating to equality which numbered 17 (5.9%) and in particular amongst the pupils these related to freedom of belief.

This is entirely consistent with the first of the two core values identified in the consultation strand of valuing ourselves and valuing others. In terms of the task of this project it is clear that the culture of the school is particularly important in promoting these values, and thus promoting spiritual, moral, social and cultural development. This will be developed in greater depth later.

Valuing Learning and Growth

The most significant family of constructs however, were those relating to learning, achievement and excellence. For pupils the language used tended to be, for example, 'trying your best' or 'working hard'. In total 65 (22.7%) of constructs appeared to be related to this idea and most were positive at the emergent pole. It appears that this sample of the population positively value learning and growth. Interestingly this did not appear in the consultation process, rather the governors added in the value of 'fulfilling our potential' as one which is central to the purpose of the school and to the Christian tradition and which could justifiably promoted as a 'good' even if pupils themselves did not value it.

Another interesting comment at this point is that this same construct group appeared the most in the staff constructs. Of the 62 constructs elicited from this group 14 (22.6%) related to achieving excellence, or the central role of learning and development. It is appropriate here to ask the question of whether what teachers value in practice actually influences what pupils value. If this is the case, then there are clearly important implications for spiritual, moral, social and cultural development. The personal constructs, or values of teachers in relation to schooling will have public implications for the education of their pupils, and especially their pupils' own value development. Research findings from a pilot project (Deakin Crick and Prosser 1996) indicate that there is a link between teachers' values and those of their pupils.

Valuing the Christian Tradition

Of the total number of pupils' constructs there were 34 (11.9%) which related to the Christian faith in some way. Of these 16 (5.6%) appeared to indicate that the Christian faith was important to the self; 12 (4.2%) appeared to indicate that it was important to the school; 1 was negative at the emergent pole; and 5 were countered by the perceived need to be tolerant of other faiths. This finding is interesting because, like learning and achievement, it did not feature significantly in the consultation on values. In fact the value of 'faith in Christ' was promoted by the governing body as one which can be justified by the fact that the foundation of the school is a Christian one.

In general it is possible to say that pupils at the school appear to be positively aware of the school's foundation, generally viewing it as an important tradition which legitimately influences the 'way things are' in the school and which can be meaningful for pupils in terms of their own faith and in terms of moral development or 'learning how to live'.

Moral Development

Another recognisable family of constructs related to moral development or knowing right from wrong. 25 (8.8%) of the total number of constructs fell into this category. Terms like 'learning how to behave well' or 'encouraging good morals' indicated that this sample of pupils were aware of the area of moral development. From the findings of this project there appears to be plenty of evidence that they are able to participate in the discussion of values and spiritual, moral, social and cultural development articulately and with some legitimate contributions to make as stakeholders.

Valuing the Environment

Pupils appeared to be keenly aware of the environment in which they worked. 26 (9.1%) of the constructs related to the school buildings, to the impact of space or lack of it, or as another example, to the need to clear up after themselves.

Valuing the curriculum

Constructs relating to the curriculum itself were scarce (3 (1.1%)) and of these the emphasis was on the breadth and variety of the curriculum or choice of subjects. There were a number of constructs which fell into other categories which indicated an awareness of the need for all round development, not purely academic development.

6. Teachers and Staff

The constructs elicited from the teachers and staff indicated a rich and diverse set of teaching and learning world views. As with the pupils, account should be taken of the fact that the elements were provided for them and thus the results simply indicate the ways in which these teachers and staff construe those elements of school which appear to be of significance to the senior management team.

Most significant values

Since these constructs were rated and then subject to a correlation statistic it is possible to identify the dominant (most used) constructs of each of the sample of teachers and staff. These are shown in table five below.

Table 5

Emergent Pole	Contrast Pole
feeling part of the school	doing the minimum
developing the whole child	inhibiting development
good academic education	unbalanced education
knowing what's right in each situation	complete disregard for rules
maintaining a balance in building to create a right environment	disorganised
all children achieving	lack of motivation
displaying lots of creative ideas	unwillingness to try new ideas and make mistakes
holistic education	narrow minded education
encountering new ideas	stagnating

The teachers and staff chosen for this sample were identified to represent as wide a spectrum of the whole body of adults working in the school as possible. They were not chosen as 'culture bearers' but simply because of their roles. Clearly there is a rich range of motivations present amongst this group of people reflecting a positive, happy and developing school culture.

A further exploration of some of the families of constructs which were identified from the whole set will offer a greater degree of understanding and possible identification of issues pertaining to this project, which aims to facilitate change and improvement in a particular area of the school life.

Valuing excellence

The most significant family of constructs related to the area of learning and achievement. Of the total of 62 constructs 14 (22.6%) related directly to excellence or achievement in pupil learning, and many of those were explicitly inclusive of children of all abilities. There was an awareness of the environment being conducive to learning and learning being relevant and enjoyable.

Valuing the whole child

Linked with the notion of learning and achievement was a distinct emphasis on social and moral development which takes account of more than just the academic aspects of the curriculum. For one teacher a 'holistic education' was the emergent pole of the construct with a 'narrow minded education' being at the contrast pole. Another example was an emergent pole of 'children developing morally, socially and academically' with a contrast pole of 'only developing academically'. Of these there were 6 (9.7%) although when taken with the emphasis on learning including all pupils picture of the culture of 'inclusive' and 'holistic' education is strengthened.

Valuing positive interpersonal relations and teamwork

Taken together these two themes could be identified in 9 (14.5%) of the total number of constructs which directly referred to ideas surrounding caring relationships between pupils and teachers, or positive partnerships with parents, or working together. This is in keeping with both the evidence of the pupils' constructs and the consultation on values where the importance of relationships became apparent as perhaps the most widely shared school value.

Valuing equality and the environment

Consistent with the emphasis on the whole child, was an emphasis on education meeting the needs of all pupils regardless of ability. Constructs directly expressing this orientation totalled 7 (11.3%). Constructs relating to caring for the environment of the school totalled 11 (17.7%) and usually there was a connection made between a positive environment, including space and resources, being an important factor to encouraging learning.

Valuing the Christian foundation of the school

The personal constructs of this sample of the population indicate that there is a very specific awareness of the Christian foundation of the school. A total of 8 (12.9%) constructs in some way referred to the Christian foundation of the school. 'Being a Christian community' or 'Christian values' were good examples. One in particular referred to the 'historically religious ethos of the school' at the emergent pole and the contrast pole was 'the hypocrisy of the school's historical background' which made reference to the historical slave and tobacco trade which took place in precisely the geographical area of the school. These constructs were not unproblematic. For example one construct was carefully worded to make a connection between the Christian foundation and moral guidance as distinct from a sense of imposing Christian beliefs. Another construct had resistance to the school's Christian ethos as its contrast pole.

The constructs relating to the Christian foundation of the school appeared to be connected with mood or ethos, and with moral values, and being a Christian community. Of particular note was a construct labelled 'a Christian framework' with a contrast pole of 'an agnostic framework. When rated against the elements it was highly associated with parents, children's creativity, teachers, children of all abilities, but it was rated as not particularly associated with history, science, displays of work or music. In other words it seems from these constructs that the Christian foundation of the school is perceived to be important because it is the historical foundation, and because it has an influence on the ethos, values and mood of the school, but not particularly relevant to the content of what is taught. If this is the case, then the requirements of this project to develop a whole school policy for spiritual, moral, social and cultural development which includes the content of the curriculum is likely to be a challenging and possibly disputed area for teachers.

Valuing the Curriculum

A similar pattern appears when exploring the constructs relating to the curriculum. In fact there were 5 (8.1%) constructs that related to the curriculum and these tended to relate to the breadth and scope of the curriculum rather than the content of what was taught. A broad curriculum was a good one, a narrow curriculum was a bad one. One construct related to particular categories of the mind. The absence of any construct relating to the content of the curriculum is again significant, posing questions that pertain significantly to the whole project.

Teachers have been the recipients of considerable educational changes over the last twenty years and the curriculum has become heavily prescribed. This finding may simply reflect the fact that many teachers perceive the content of the curriculum as a 'given', something over which they have no control. It may also be that the dominant liberal view of knowledge, where values are separate from facts, and real learning has to do with the 'hard facts' may be another reason why the content of the curriculum does not appear consciously in these teaching and learning worldviews. Similarly a focus on process rather than content will render the content unproblematic, or insignificant. In any event given that this project is engaged with the question of how values and spiritual, moral, social and cultural development occurs within schemes of work, amongst other aspects of school life, then this is a finding which warrants further investigation.

7. Conclusions

Thus, overall, the investigation of personal constructs amongst pupils, teachers and staff yielded much of interest and significance for the first step of this project. It confirmed and supported the findings of the values consultation strand, highlighting the importance that both pupils and teachers place on positive relationships. It highlighted too, that what pupils and teachers appear to value highly in this school is learning and achievement for all pupils, not just those with academic orientation. It raised the question of the meaning and scope of the school's Christian foundation, and identified the area of the content of the curriculum as one needing significant attention and coherent and relevant treatment when it comes to developing a whole school policy for spiritual, moral, social and cultural development.

Chapter Four
School Ethos and Climate

1. Introduction

The term 'ethos' is perhaps one of the most vague and ill-defined words in use in education. Never the less the 'ethos' of the school is something that parents, teachers and pupils consider to be important. How people feel and think about the place they learn and teach in makes a difference to how they do their job. 'This is a really good place to learn/teach' is a view that matters, and makes a difference to the ways in which people grow and develop within the institution. Pupils and teachers are quick to identify practices that do not measure up to the espoused values of the organisation, and will make judgements about policies and practices which are rooted in their own histories, feelings and intuitions as well as in the rational merits of a policy or practice.

2. Lived values – whole people

Core values, then, are lived as well as taught. Truth, justice, valuing others, or any other of those core ethical values which recur as ideals within schools and communities, are expressed through action and behaviour as well as through rational definition and through human aspiration. They are polyvalent in their meaning and in their application and are they are not 'free floating' concepts that are divorced from human history, and the stories that make up the lives of individuals in schools. Indeed, in an explicit or implicit manner, they constitute the 'life world' of schools.

The commitment of individual teachers and leaders in school to personal development and growth makes an important contribution to the 'ethos' of the school. People who are emotionally closed, unable to take responsibility for their own feelings and responses and who always locate problems at everybody else's door, do not encourage the sort of open learning community in which spiritual and moral development can be fostered. Willingness to acknowledge mistakes, to take personal responsibility for change and commitment to open communication with the other are all important foundations for ethically healthy schools. Children, especially, are tuned in to lack of congruence in adults and will respond positively to teachers who are authentic, respectful and warm. Rogers argues that the three conditions for (Rogers and Stevens. 1973) personal growth in 'becoming more fully human' are

- Unconditional positive regard
- Authenticity
- Empathy

It may be that these three factors are also critical conditions for learning and growth of all sorts, including in schools where the process of 'humanisation' is never far from vision. If the basic conditions for growth are in place in children's lives then learning is something a bit like growing. It happens.

3. Values, Narratives and Worldviews

The core values identified in the case study school were consciously rooted into a particular belief system or worldview - that of the Judeo-Christian tradition. All values are rooted into belief systems of some sort - they are not independent and separate from facts, worldviews, ideologies, attitudes and beliefs, feelings, histories and life scripts. In contemporary society there are many values which will be shared at some level by all worldviews, ideologies and belief systems, although the source of those values may be different. For example all but one of the case study school's values are likely to be shared by all worldviews and most religions, but their interpretation and the ways in which they cohere into an overall story will be different in a secular, Jewish, Islamic, Sikh, Steiner or Christian school. An understanding of the larger narratives, or worldview frameworks, within which differing core values cohere, provides an important critical framework for discussion and debate in schools, between schools and in the wider plural society. Rather than seeing ideologies, or worldviews as impediments to education, which have to be left behind at the door of the learning institution, an appropriately critical understanding of the notion that no individual or institution or community approaches learning from a 'value neutral' perspective will enhance learning. This is because worldview frameworks, with their inherent narratives and explanations, provide an important strategy for the critical assimilation of knowledge because they provide a system within which new information can be located and made meaningful. They may well enhance the skills of critical thinking in the field of spiritual, moral, social and cultural development as well as critical thinking in and between the disciplines themselves. An understanding of the larger worldviews or narratives, which shape contemporary culture, may also be an important means of educating for meaning and purpose, and a vehicle through which young learners can begin to identify their own worldview commitments and values.

4. Whose spirituality, whose values, whose narratives?

The set of values known as the SCAA values, which arose from the National Forum for Values in Education and the Community during 1996, represented a significant consensus on the sorts of values which schools could and should be promoting and nurturing in young people. Despite a great deal of debate and scepticism, and much mis-understanding, taken at face value, that consultation was a significant landmark in education policy. It indicated that there were ethical values which society believed to be important, that were to some extent shared, and that schools could confidently articulate and utilise in their curriculum and organisation. This was significant for a profession where the idea of indoctrination was, and still is, the antithesis of education, and where the notion of allowing young people to come to their own judgements about spiritual and moral issues was and still is, an important value in itself for many in the teaching profession.

What the SCAA forum did not do, purposely, was to engage in debate about the source of those values - about the belief systems, worldviews, ideologies within which those values can be located. The fact was, and still is, that there would be no consensus about any one worldview, belief system or ideology as the appropriate one to inform schooling and education. Contemporary society is plural in terms of the belief systems and faith commitments to which its communities adhere, at least at a personal and private level. In public life, there has been more uniformity – with the discourses of economism, technicism and utilitarianism powerfully shaping experience in public institutions.

The situation is a complex one, and cannot be approached in a simplistic manner. Schools and individuals are influenced from a range of sources and narrow-minded 'fundamentalism' is not the prerogative of the religious. The 'tolerance' of the liberal can be as oppressive of faith and other perspectives as sometimes the religious can be damning of the 'secular'. In educational institutions the notion of openness, dialogue and respecting difference are key dispositions for ethical health. The consensus of the local school community is perhaps the healthiest means of answering the question of 'whose values' should schools promote, always providing that there is space for critique, questioning and dialogue.

5. Values as organising principles

In the case study school, the particular understanding of the nature of core values, as elaborated here, provided a means of integrating a whole school approach to the spiritual, moral, social and cultural development of pupils and to citizenship education. A set of, in this case, nine core values, owned and articulated by the community provided a powerful integrating and interdisciplinary vehicle for organising a whole school framework. At the heart of any school is its distinctive vision and values. That vision, significantly expressed in its core values, can be articulated and practised in all aspects of school life and organisation, and thus it can be monitored, evaluated and reviewed.

To summarise some key ideas about values, arising from work in the case study school:

- Each of the school's core values has a spiritual, moral, social and cultural aspect to it. (see diagram)

- These core values cohere within a larger narrative worldview framework.

- Most of the values will be shared by most of society and therefore also by teachers and pupils who do not share the Christian faith.

- Dialogue is a key modus operandi for values education, rather than precise philosophical or religious definitions agreed within a community.

Core values have spiritual, moral, social and cultural dimensions which find expression throughout the curriculum.

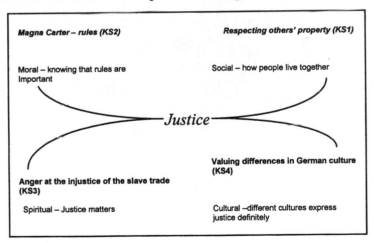

Magna Carter – rules (KS2)   *Respecting others' property (KS1)*

Moral – knowing that rules are   Social – how people live together
Important

Justice

Valuing differences in German culture
(KS4)

Anger at the injustice of the slave trade (KS3)

Spiritual – Justice matters   Cultural –different cultures express
justice definitely

Diagram to show some of the spiritual, moral, social and cultural dimensions of the value of justice

6. The location of values in school organisation

The following diagram, drawn from various sources, indicates the central place which a school's vision and values have in determining the ethos, or the climate of the school, and thus the nature of the spiritual, moral, social and cultural development of pupils;

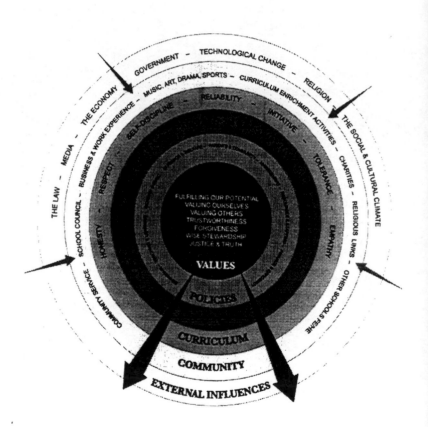

7. Whole School Policies

In developing new policies, or in reviewing existing ones, a critical question has to do with the manner in which the policy itself is consistent with, and expresses particular aspects of the school's vision and core values. This is more than simply a paper exercise, and can lead to serious professional reflection on both theory and practice that in turn can lead to improvement and change. For example, many schools will value the child as a unique individual, worth, of care, consideration, nurture and equal access to learning opportunities. In developing teaching and learning policies in such schools, the question is how does our approach to teaching and learning reflect what we value about the learner? Does it take into account, for example, multiple intelligence theory with its maxim of 'how are you smart?' rather than 'how smart are you?' Does it take into account the notion of preferred learning styles? How does the school's approach to assessment actually promote learning? What sort of critical engagement with knowledge does our teaching strategy aim for? The ways in which a school answers these questions has implications for the school's approach to differentiation, to assessment and reporting and to the role of teacher – as instructor, facilitator of learning, guide or transmitter of facts. Each key school policy can be subject to critical questions in this way and the authority for change is not located in the government, the LEA, or the whim of the headteacher, but in the distinctive vision and values of this particular learning community. That vision provides a third critical voice in the dilemmas of policy making and change in schools.

The school's vision and core values should be evident in:

- The vision and mission statement
- Strategic aims and objectives
- All key policies
- Subject area policies
- Schemes of work
- The quality of relationships within the community.

- Teaching and learning strategies
- Lesson planning and assessment
- The rituals, customs, symbols, imagery and structure of school life
- The management structures of the school
- Prospectus/Publicity
- Staff Induction/Student Induction

The Silence of the Curriculum

Throughout the case study, in the consultation and the investigation, an overwhelming silence pervaded any discussion about values and the content of the curriculum. Values were understood to be present in the culture of the school, its organisational practices and in the quality of relationships, but as far as the curriculum was concerned, there was silence.

One explanation of this is that the curriculum is seen increasingly to be a 'given', something imposed by government through the National Curriculum, which leaves very little room for teacher discretion and therefore change or adaptation. Teachers have been overwhelmed with changes throughout the years of reform, and those changes pervade the 'what' and the 'how' questions of teaching and learning, leaving very little space for the 'why' questions. At a very basic level, teachers could be seen to be mere technicians of the government's agenda – which is a very subtle but powerful form of de-professionalisation.

A second explanation is that teachers trained in the second half of the 20th century have been powerfully influenced by the thinking of educationalists who themselves have been shaped by the ideas and thought forms of modernity, with its focus on rationality, and its separation of fact from value. Hirst and Peters,(Hirst 1974) more or less standard reading in teacher training colleges for many years, developed an approach to knowledge which explicitly set up the rationality of each form of knowledge as the final arbiter in human affairs, and argued that religious belief was irrelevant to the forms of knowledge and thus to the subjects of the curriculum. The belief, therefore, in the neutrality of the curriculum has a powerful pedigree in custom and practice. Values, beliefs, and spiritual and moral development have all been conveniently relegated to the private and the personal, leaving the public domain of knowledge and the curriculum devoid of such critique, and fragmented into segments of knowledge without a coherent way of putting it all together.

These views are no longer tenable – the myth of neutrality in the curriculum has been shown to be unsupportable. Bottery (Bottery 1990) argues a strong case for the dependency of facts upon values and of values upon facts. One cannot for example make a serious evaluation about foetal research or nuclear deterrence without knowing the factual background. However at the same time the notion that there are facts that are solid, permanent and unchangeable is a popular myth that needs to be challenged if values are to be dealt with fully within education. Historical 'facts' for example are selected because of prior values about what is important. "Facts' are plucked from obscurity to fame because of their contribution to an overall scheme' (ibid p47). The area of scientific enquiry is also dependent upon a prior scheme of values, which poses the questions as well as the hypotheses and selects which facts are important and which are not. There are serious criticisms of the objectivity of the methodology of scientific enquiry ((Kuhn 1970) (Feyerabend 1975) (Lakatos 1978; Polanyi 1958; Popper 1970)which render it less than purely objective. Indeed it would rest somewhere between Bottery's classification of personal and social levels of objectivity. He claims that there is no area of human knowledge that can claim ·to have total objectivity - science and all other areas of knowledge are at best tentative and changeable.

Even mathematics, which has traditionally been viewed as the paradigm of certain knowledge, consisting of absolute and unchallengeable truths, has been subject to severe criticism. Ernest (Ernest 1991) discusses the relationship between philosophy and mathematics and proposes the view that mathematical truth is fallible and corrigible, and can never be regarded as beyond revision and correction. He then goes on to show how different educational ideologies promote different views of mathematics, and in turn these lead to often very different teaching and learning styles, schemes of work, and curricular materials within the area of mathematics.

Given the silence from the teachers in relation to values and the curriculum in the case study school, the project went on to focus on the curriculum itself, rather than on other aspects of school life. It is to the curriculum that we turn in chapter five.

Chapter Five
A Focus on the Curriculum

1. Introduction

Having gone through an extended process of determining what core values the schools as a community believed were important, the research team turned its attention to the curriculum. The question was, what difference did this school's vision and values make to the ways in which history was taught, or how did the specific vision of, for example, the science department reflect and enhance the whole school's vision and values? The fact that the team knew that the pupils believed these values to be important, as did their teachers, parents and governors, was a significant factor that provided an important building block in the development process. It answered the important question of 'whose values' can we legitimately nurture in this school.

A very significant part of pupils' experience in school takes place in relation to the taught curriculum, which is central to the purpose of the school. For this to be uninfluenced by the school's vision and core values is a significant gap – though one that is commonplace and often unexamined. Indeed what actually goes on in the classroom, in terms of formal expectations of teaching and learning, makes a powerful statement to pupils about what is of real value in this community.

2. Curriculum Audit

In the case study school, the research team undertook a curriculum audit in relation to the relevance of the schools' core values. Each department identified a member of staff who worked with a research teacher to examine the content of the schemes of work in that subject area. This entailed a discussion about the key idea of teaching and learning with a values focus in the subject. Then followed an interrogation of the content of what was taught to identify where, if at all, there were moments of opportunity to focus teaching and learning on the school's core values.

3.   Spirituality and the Curriculum

A number of interesting findings emerged from this process. Firstly the concept of the school's values being implicit in the subjects was readily accepted by all teachers, who understood and were enthusiastic about the approach. The teachers' enthusiasm always emerged when the discussion arrived at the question of the real value of their particular subject and its purpose. In other words when the question of 'why' teach science, or history or maths, came into the foreground, so did the teacher's sense of personal vocation and vision. For example, the idea that geography is intrinsically about how human society is organised in relation to the natural world and that this is laden with overarching values, such as stewardship and justice, was an idea which was not new. However it suddenly gained new legitimacy as a potential vehicle for spiritual, moral, social and cultural development of pupils and citizenship. Similarly science was seen to be essentially about a search for truth in the natural world, which could rarely be undertaken without reference to many of the school's core values, such as stewardship, or trust.

If spirituality is 'the developing relationship of the individual, within community and tradition, to that which is - or is perceived to be - of ultimate concern, ultimate value and ultimate truth' then these aspects of each subject become sites for the promotion of spirituality as a basic human quality. The nature of that spirituality, with differing underlying assumptions, may vary from community to community, but there is likely to be a significant degree of consensus in the actual ideal. The interconnection between a search for truth and the task of science is difficult to deny from any perspective, but educational discourse about truth in science can only be enhanced by the fact that differing worldviews may offer differing perspectives on the nature of that truth. How those perspectives are respected is, of course, critical to ethical education. Narrow-mindedness and dogmatism in this domain are not the prerogative of the religious – indeed often religious schools and religious teachers are more sensitive to difference than their 'secular counterparts'. This may be because they have not had the privilege of 'dominant status' in the academy that has been enjoyed for so long by secular liberal perspectives and thus have become more sensitive to intolerance and the human need for respect.

4. Three Modes of Values in the Curriculum

Secondly it became clear through the audit process that the school's values appeared in different clusters in different subject areas, although all of the school's values appeared somewhere in all of the subjects. However some subjects appeared to stand in a different relation to values than others. It was clear that the school's values appeared in at least three different modes within the curriculum:

a) *Intrinsic to the teaching and learning process or pedagogy*

The processes of teaching and learning involve relationships, and social organisation. Discussion in class requires that all participants are valued, fieldwork requires trust, mistakes require forgiveness, taking turns requires fairness, relationships require respect and truth, and so on.

b) *Intrinsic to the information content*

The information content of learning about the social or the natural world cannot be encountered without implicit or ·explicit reference to core values. For example learning French cannot take place without developing an attitude of some sort towards 'the other' or people of different culture and language. Maths is intrinsically about the discovery of truth and intricate relationships in the natural world. History has to do with the search for truth in how human society has organised itself and developed over time – which is laden with all human values.

c) *Intrinsic to the application of the subject*

Values are always implicit in the application of an area of knowledge or skill to another aspect of life. For example, technology is the application of science to human culture and as such is laden with questions of values. Whether it is related to the source of raw materials (how they are made, who benefits from them) or to the human use of the artefact or technology, questions of valuing others, justice, stewardship and other values are always present. Maths is applied in many forms – its use in statistics is one example of where it is important to discern truth from falsehood – and in the classroom the subject matter of what the maths is applied to can be heavily value laden.

These three modes of values in the curriculum are consistent with the understanding of core values, or 'virtues' as entities which are ' lived in community' and 'in relationship' and understood within a narrative perspective, as well as entities which can be understood and developed intellectually. The rituals, symbols, routines and processes of daily life, and of classroom life, all tell a story about that which is of value, or worth. The experience of fairness or indeed of unfairness, gives a learner a lived concept about which she or he can then think and these core values do, actually matter to learners. Without coherence between experience, culture and learning there is less capacity to understand and learn and apply that learning.

Developmentally, 'living within' a value framework comes prior to an intellectual understanding and critique of that value framework, and it may even be that the latter is dependent on the former. Understanding of one's own value framework is an important prerequisite to changing it, or to understanding and respecting another's value framework.

5.   The scope of values across the curriculum

It is clear that values can be targeted specifically within the curriculum across all subjects. From the examples documented in table form for year seven in the case study school, which are similar to years eight and nine, it is clear that certain values appear more readily with certain subjects in the views of those teachers engaged in the audit work. The following table shows this.

Subject	Most frequent Values	Mode
Maths	Truth, Awe and Wonder, Stewardship/justice Valuing self and others Fulfilling potential	Content Application Pedagogy
Geography	Stewardship Justice Valuing others Valuing self Trust Fulfilling potential	Content Pedagogy
History	Truth Justice/valuing others Faith in Christ Valuing ourselves	Content Pedagogy
Science	Truth - trusting the community of scientists Fulfilling potential Justice Stewardship Valuing self and others	Content Application Pedagogy
DT	Justice Stewardship Valuing self Valuing others Fulfilling potential	Application Pedagogy
Personal and Social Education	All except faith in Christ	Content Application Pedagogy
Religious Education	All, including faith in Christ	Content Application Pedagogy

6.   Content and method in spiritual, moral, social and cultural development

An important distinction in spiritual and moral development, or values education using this methodology is that between content and method. Very often spiritual development is linked with process ideas, such as inviting learners to experience 'awe and wonder' or to engage in 'silent personal reflection'. These processes are important components of spiritual and moral development but they are simply processes and do not give any indication of content. It is quite possible that learners could feel so impressed at the skill and achievements of Adolf Hitler that they might be pleased to silently reflect on this, or perhaps on the latest scenes of football hooliganism from the news the night before. The point is that process alone is not enough and it relates only to age appropriate teaching and learning strategies which encourage spiritual and moral development. The school's values framework provides some substantive content for that process to focus on, which has the authority of consensus within the community as well as relevance to learners.

The values content in the curriculum is open and dialogical in nature because core values such as truth, or justice are guiding principles rather than 'dogmatic rules' or 'lists of do's and don'ts, and always require interpretation in their application to experience. There are undoubtedly times when teachers and parents will wish to be unequivocal in their application of certain values to certain subjects – for example few will condone child abuse, or murder, or planned violence, or the extermination of ethnic groups. However in general terms there are always a variety of factors to be taken into account, and many possible interpretations in practice in values education. It is the quality of discourse that matters in educative settings, and the shared intention to be reflective and purposeful in the application of certain core values to life that is significant in a community.

Thus core values provide a means of examining the ethical aspects of the content of the curriculum, which is itself evaluative and requires reasoning and enquiry skills, creative thinking skills and the ability to process information and locate it within a wider framework. This is not a precise science: it is more of an interpretative task. However it is possible to produce SMART (specific, measurable, achievable, realistic, time related) targets for spiritual and moral development within the whole curriculum and to be explicit about content, process and desirable outcomes in terms of pupil skills, dispositions and attitudes. This will be looked at in more depths in later chapters.

7. Core Values and Systems Thinking in the Curriculum

One of the outcomes of a scientific technological worldview is the reduction of the curriculum into a virtually infinite assortment of discrete facts, each with its precise definition. Knowledge is reduced to the accumulation of facts, intelligence is a fixed and measurable entity, and learning has to do with memory and recall and so on. Harman (Harman 1988) refers to this as 'the science of the parts' which he argues is no longer appropriate on its own for the 21st century, and that we need to develop the 'science of whole systems'. Kegan (Kegan 1994) argues that the world is moving rapidly to a 'stick-shift' culture, away from an 'automatic' culture. In an automatic culture traditions and social structures largely determine peoples' life trajectories, whereas in a 'stick-shift' culture individuals have greater freedom and the responsibility to shape their own lives. As a result of globalisation, information and communications technology and cheap transportation, people are experiencing the mix of diverse cultures and value systems and need to engage more and more with complex uncertainties and opportunities. What is increasingly clear is that learning how to learn is a key life-skill for the 21st century, and a significant part of learning how to learn is understanding systems thinking, or making connections between discrete items of information and locating learning within a meaningful worldview framework.

Introducing core values into the teaching and learning process and exploring questions of values as they pertain to the content of science, geography or maths, brings learners into contact with the *context* of their learning, or the big picture. This is the essence of systems thinking. Understanding a wider worldview or values framework enhances learning by facilitating students in making connections between otherwise fragmented data, between disciplines and, significantly, between school learning and 'real life'.

A school's vision and core values provide a means of curriculum coherence that facilitates learners in making meaning out of school and learning. The core values of the case study school, embedded within a particular worldview, have certain implications for knowledge and learning, and certain built in assumptions that are relevant to both the content and the process of learning. To adequately engage in values education within a discipline requires the learner to locate the problem in science, or geography within a wider worldview framework, which includes ideas about a 'hoped for future' and analysis about what is problematic in the way things are. It engages the learner in critical thinking, creative thinking and draws upon different forms of intelligence, particularly inter-personal, intra-personal and perspectival intelligence as well as those intelligences required by the subject content. The learner understands that, science, for example, does not take place in a vacuum, but is located within history and community and is both fallible and can be used for good or bad ends.

The identity of a school community within a particular tradition – be that religious or 'secular' – and the location of values education in critical dialogue with that tradition brings an immediacy to learning and can also stimulate a vision for institutional and social change. The tradition within which the learner is located is immediate, tangible and experienced and sometimes already found wanting by the learner. Values questions most often occur when there are problems which require critical reflection on the way things are done, and a localised and critical engagement with a tradition is an important aspect of citizenship education. Within a religious tradition critique and dialogue is an important strategy for healthy organisations and a means of revitalisation.

8. Plurality and Shared Values – structure and direction

The 1996 SCAA consultation provided evidence that there is broad consensus in the UK amongst people of all faiths and none in certain basic values that are considered essential for healthy individuals and communities. Further work by Kidder (Kidder 1994) who interviewed leading thinkers, artists, writers, educators, business people and religious and political leaders from around the world arrived at similar conclusions. Kidder identifies eight universal values necessary to create the moral conditions for a sustainable 21st century – love, truthfulness, fairness, freedom, unity, tolerance, responsibility and respect for life.

Core values such as these and the set arrived through consultation in the case study school are relatively easy to negotiate. The authority of consensus is important, but it does not deal with the underlying worldviews and belief systems that inform these values. It does not deal with the source of those values. This is where the reality of pluralism begins to emerge. In fact the reasons why different individuals and communities value 'human life' can vary significantly. For example a theistic worldview offers the belief, or the truth claim, that human beings are valued because they are 'made in the image of God'. On the other hand a humanistic worldview offers the belief or truth claim that human beings are valued because they are the highest form of life on earth. These ultimate beliefs, shared within differing communities, offer a 'directional co-ordinate' to core values, or a distinctive perspective which can shape the content and process of spiritual and moral development in relation to those values.

9. Perspectival approaches to values

In the case study school, the core values, excluding 'faith in Christ' represented a way of **structuring** spiritual, moral, social and cultural development that is possibly generic, and certainly will be common to many schools. However the Faith in Christ value represented the **directional co-ordinate** for the other values, or a perspectival approach to the core values. This enables teachers to introduce discussions about a Christian perspective on justice, or truth into lessons, where appropriate and in an educatively defensible manner. Alternative perspectives can also be used educatively – indeed for pupils to learn that there are existing defensible alternative perspectives on values is of critical importance as they grow into a world which is diverse, fluid and mixed in terms of values and communities. The same argument applies for a religious school of another faith, or for a school with a 'secular' worldview and value system. Spiritual and moral development can take place with reference to core values in all types of schools because spirituality and morality are inherent within core values, by definition. Whether the type of spirituality a school promotes is a particular religious spirituality or whether it is an anthropological spirituality, or an eclectic mixture, is the choice of that school and its community.

10. Personal Social and Health Education and Religious Education are central

From the curriculum audit in the case study school it was clear that Personal and Social and Health Education and Religious Education stand in a different relationship to values than do the other subjects covered. Both Religious Education and Personal and Social and Health Education deal with all of the core values in all of the three modes consistently, although again 'faith in Christ' as a core value emerged as distinctive by its absence in PSHE and by its pervasive presence in RE.

Religious Education is about values from a theological perspective and Personal and Social and Health Education is about values from a 'lived' or 'personal and social' perspective. In terms of a 'values contribution' to the curriculum these two subjects have a very significant place. The point is that 'doing justice' is relevant personally and socially and theologically as well as being relevant to science, or French and it is the specific task of RE and PSHE to open up that relevance to pupils.

11. Citizenship Education and Core Values

Citizenship education can make a new and important contribution to values across the curriculum. The QCA defines the three interrelated strands that should run through all citizenship education, at all Key Stages, as;

- Social and moral responsibility
- Community involvement
- Political literacy

These are delivered in three modes throughout the curriculum:

- Discrete citizenship provision with separate curriculum time
- Teaching citizenship within and through other subjects, curriculum areas and courses.
- Citizenship events, activities and tutorial work.

What is clear about the citizenship agenda is that it is designed to be far more than a discrete body of knowledge delivered through a particular period on the timetable. The essential elements of citizenship education included a number of key, overarching concepts, a set of spiritual and moral values and character dispositions, skills and aptitudes and knowledge and understanding which is contextualised in the life experience of the learners.

Citizenship can be approached from the perspective of the curriculum – a focus on what is to be taught on the timetable, from the perspective of the 'ethos' of the school, or from a professional transformational approach. This latter approach requires a whole school strategy, addressing all aspects of school life, including the curriculum. It depends centrally on teacher professional development in relation to integrating personal development with academic development across the curriculum.

This whole school vision for citizenship overlaps significantly with the strategies for values education outlined in this book since much of citizenship education addresses core values from a political and social perspective. Indeed, there is nearly always a political dimension to questions of values within the content of the curriculum, and there is also often scope for development into community involvement or service learning. Sunderland C., Deakin Crick R and Peskelt D, et al (2001) have developed a conceptual framework for citizenship education which utilises four key concepts as essential conceptual tools for a transformational approach to citizenship. These are:

- The concept of story or narrative as key ways in which humans in community know what they know
- The concept of trust or human co-operation as central to community
- The concept science and society – how human communities use knowledge
- The concept of power and motivation as central to understanding society

These conceptual tools are powerful means of addressing questions of values across the curriculum, enabling a more indepth and rigorous consideration of the content of citizenship education than may otherwise occur within the curriculum.

As with Religious and Personal, Social and Health Education, Citizenship Education does include a discrete body of knowledge, skills and understanding which demands planned curriculum time, even though it makes a unique contribution to values across the curriculum. Whether human rights or the economic system as topics of study appear in history or geography or in a new period called citizenship is not so important as that these types of topics are planned and taught with care and rigour. In practice the logistic demands of time-tabling and other pressures indicate that it is highly likely that much of the taught components of citizenship will appear in humanities, and that PSHE and Citizenship may well share space on the secondary school timetable over the year. The options in the primary school are more fluid, given the different structure of the school and the less demanding citizenship PSHE agenda.

The next chapter will look in more detail at the teaching and learning implications of values education across the curriculum.

Chapter Six
Teaching and Learning

1. Research Question

During the second year of the research project, five teachers developed teaching and learning interventions which focused on the school's core values as specific learning objectives within their subjects, which were science, geography, music, Religious Education and French. Their particular aim was to find out whether planned lesson interventions which promoted learning and reflection about the schools values changed the way in which pupils perceived those values in relation to science, music, RE, geography and french?

Changes in the ways in which pupils perceived the school's core values were argued to be consistent with the notion of positive development if the pupils increased in their understanding of the relevance of those values to a particular subject. An increased pupil use of the core values in relation to the taught curriculum was argued to be consistent with the notion of spiritual, moral, social and cultural development of pupils within that subject. This is because the school's core values were deemed to have spiritual, moral, social and cultural aspects to them, which are difficult to separate out, and which are present in potential in any serious reflection on those values in their application to the social and natural world.

The purpose was to find out whether teaching about values in a planned and integrated way across a range of subjects would encourage an understanding, appreciation and personal ·interpretation of those values.

2. Research aims:

- To design and implement teaching and learning strategies that intentionally promoted an understanding of the school's core values as learning objectives within lesson plans.

- To measure the ways in which pupils understood the school's values in relation to the taught curriculum.
- To assess the effect of the delivery of these lessons on the ways pupils' understood the school's values in relation to the subjects.
- To review the impact on curriculum design and implementation of teaching and learning strategies to promote spiritual, moral, social and cultural development through the school's cores values within the whole curriculum.
- To assess the reactions and responses of teachers involved in lesson design and values interpretation on the classroom.

3. Developing and evaluating values interventions

At the beginning of the year the research team held a working session with colleagues from their subject specialisms to examine their forthcoming schemes of work and to identify where opportunities for values education might occur, and the sorts of teaching strategies which might be employed to facilitate this. The following diagram indicates the ways in which the team understood values to be present in the curriculum.

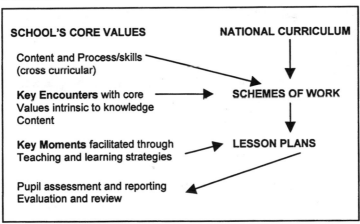

The teachers then devised a series of lesson plans which covered a range of topics over a period of two terms in which they would deliver these values interventions, making them specific learning objectives within their lesson planning. They expected to cover all of the school's values during the period of the experiment. In most cases pupils completed written work, in class or as homework, which enabled the teachers to form an assessment of the effect of the interventions. The teachers also completed their own observations and evaluations on a fieldwork pro forma and these were designed to be available for analysis by the whole team

The teachers held three formal focus group discussions during the course of the experimental teaching and learning strategies to identify what they perceived was actually happening in terms of pupils' learning. These discussions were chaired, and each member of the team was asked to comment on each teacher's observations. The outcomes of the discussions were minuted and returned to the teachers for further scrutiny. The discussions were recorded and analysed by one of the researchers.

In addition the deputy head and another researcher observed each teacher on two occasions during the experimental teaching and learning strategies and fed back to the focus group their observations and evaluations. On two occasions videotapes were made of the classes which were also used in the analysis.

As a result by the end of the experimental period the research team were able to identify the ways in which they perceived the experimental pupils perceptions of the school's values in relation to the subjects to have changed and to make some observations on what was actually happening in terms of teaching and learning processes during the interventions.

4. Measuring Changes in pupils' thinking about core values

In order to assess the impact of the experiment on the experimental classes each teacher selected a control class that would cover the same topics in the same subjects, but without the values interventions. Another teacher in the department taught the control classes.

At the beginning of the year both the experimental classes and the control classes were given a questionnaire which was based on the Repertory Grid Technique. This is a form of structured interview that was designed by George Kelly (1955) to elicit information about how individuals go about understanding and making sense of the world in which they live. A repertory grid is a grid whose axes are made up of elements and constructs.

Elements of the individual's world are identified (and called elements) and these can be related to any domain about which the researcher is interested in investigating. In this project the research team took key topics from the schemes of work which the pupils would be encountering during the year and made these the elements of the repertory grid.

The research team used the school's values as constructs to form the second axis of each repertory grid. Constructs are important ways of understanding the world, which have two poles (an emergent pole and a contrast pole) and involve the person's emotions, attitudes and values as well as their cognitive thought processes.

In October of that year five pupils from both the control classes and the experimental classes were asked to fill in a repertory grid questionnaire in which they rated the relevance of the school's value (or construct) against an aspect of the scheme of work on a seven point scale. The results were formed into a grid, and entered into a computer programme which then performed some statistical tests on the information which resulted in the research team being able to identify which were the most significant values (or constructs) for each pupil in relation to the subject.

After the interventions, in May of that academic year, the instrument was used again in the same way on the same pupils.

By a detailed statistical analysis which was provided by the software, the research team was able to make some judgements about changes in the ways pupils understood the school's values before and after the interventions, and to compare the experimental target pupils with the non-experimental control pupils.

5. Examples of Teaching and Learning Interventions: Science

The science classes were year eight (age 12/13) pupils in mixed sex and mixed ability groups. Both sets of pupils were of equal average ability but neither set included the most able who were taught together in another group.   During the interventions both groups studied approximately the same topics – Earth and Space, Staying Alive, Sight and Sound, Water, and Energy. The five pupils selected from each class for repertory grid analysis were taken from the range of abilities within the class, and included one pupil from a minority ethnic groups, and one pupil from a low income background, as determined by their receiving a free school meal.

a) Science Investigations / Working in Groups

This intervention took place towards the end of a number of lessons in which pupils had been engaged in a practical investigation in which they had been working in groups. In order to carry out the investigation, pupils were given the problem of finding out how a variable of their choice affected the amount of light passing through paper (e.g. colour, thickness, number of sheets etc.).   Pupils planned their investigation in groups of 2 or 3, carried out their experiments and then reported their findings.   This process took approximately 3 one-hour lessons. At the beginning of the third lesson, during the process of reporting on results, the teacher introduced the nine school values. The pupils were then asked to think about how the values were related to the investigation they had been doing, and the work they had been doing together in groups. After 10 minutes, a previously appointed spokes-person for each group shared their ideas with the class, and the teacher wrote these on the board as a brainstorm chart as they were given. Each pupil then copied the ideas into the back of their exercise books. The following is a summary of what the brainstorm contained.

- Trying to get the best possible results.
- Respecting the comments of others in the group.
- Listening to each other's ideas.
- Not cheating - God will know!
- Sharing equipment.
- Making a fair test.
- Not making up results.
- Helping each other with equipment
- Forgiving other peoples mistakes.
- Taking care of equipment.
- Trusting people to get the right equipment.

During the brainstorm there was a lot of enthusiasm to try to "get" as many of the values as possible. Hence, "not cheating - God will know". There was a good general awareness that many values were involved, and ideas came from a wide range of pupils. This process was very much an addition to the normal process of carrying out an investigation. Comments about working together would normally have been restricted to sorting out situations where pupils were not effectively working together!

b)   Science - Blood Transfusions

This intervention took place over a week, with some work done in lesson time, and some in homework time. The context was a module about certain parts of the human body, including the blood system. Pupils were first given sheet 1, giving general information about blood transfusions, blood groups and blood banks. They read each section and answered the questions that followed. The work began in a lesson and was completed for homework. The purpose of this sheet was to set the scene in terms of pupils' knowledge and understanding, and present Charles Drew, a respected pioneer in the field of blood transfusions.

The second sheet was given as a homework one week later. The purpose of this sheet was to reveal an unexpected side of the story about how Charles Drew had in fact died from loss of blood following a road traffic accident when he was refused treatment in a whites only hospital because he was black.

The response of the pupils to the second sheet was quite emotive. These emotions included sadness, anger, upset and irritation over the way in which Drew was treated because he was black, as well as happiness and admiration because of the successful things he had done.

This work was an addition to work that would normally be done on this subject, both in terms of science content and "values" content. Because some work was done as homework it did not extend the time taken to cover the unit too much.

6. French

The target groups were year 10 pupils, average ability and perhaps a little bit dissaffected with French, especially the boys. French was taught through a series of topics such as personal identification, food and drink, school and shopping. Use of conversation in the target language is encouraged and is used as far as possible. The skills of listening, speaking, reading and writing in the target language are developed through these themes. The course book used attempts to introduce a cultural element – for example study of other French speaking countries, with their differing cultural practices.

Designing values interventions for these themes was straightforward because the topics themselves deal with real life situations, although pupils do not always perceive that to be the case. For example, making a complaint in a shop in the target language was a focus for several interventions which drew upon the school's core values of valuing others, truth and forgiveness. However pupils did not appear initially to make links between this situation and their own experience of making a complaint.

a) French – geographical surroundings

One topic selected for an intervention was geographical surroundings in which pupils are normally expected to talk and write about their area, the amenities there, their opinions of the area and to increase their vocabulary related to this topic. The focus for an intervention within this topic was the creation of a new community, drawing on the history of the creation of Montreal. (Use was made of materials drawn from the Charis Project)

The pupils had to decide on the following components they wanted in their community;

➢ The buildings
➢ The occupations of the people who would be setting up the community
➢ The rules the community would live by.

One of the features of this intervention was that pupils were asked why they were choosing particular occupations and buildings. This was important because it required them to think speculatively about what is meant by a community, and what is needed to create a happy and stable community. Respecting and valuing others, and justice were the key values which emerged as important. A focus on the rules by which the community would live brought in a number of the school's core values – although not these were not referred to explicitly. Discussion was limited by the pupils' lack of sophistication in the language, and to develop deeper discussions of the values –

for example when is it OK to lie – would have meant moving into English and detracting from the lesson objectives.

Evaluation of the intervention took the form of a test and an Information Technology project, which was a summary of what had been learned. Both the French language was assessed and the level of pupil engagement with the values content. The French language work was not as accurate as would be expected of year 10 pupils because the vocabulary was new, and the teacher focus was on the values intervention itself as a research exercise. The pupils were trying to be more sophisticated in what they communicated about the topic, but lacked the equivalent level of sophistication in the language skills. Pupils were more committed to this new approach to the topic than other year ten groups. The quality of work they produced indicated that they had thought about the values issues, that they did have views of their own and that they were able to speculate about the moral and spiritual components of being a community.

b) French - Food and Drink

The Food and Drink topic normally addressed what pupils liked and disliked about food. In this intervention the teacher started in a new way by introducing foreign foods, with a combination of new and old vocabulary. This intervention focused on valuing other people and in particular valuing difference. What the teacher noticed was pupils thinking about their prejudices about foreign food and therefore foreign cultures, and being open to new ideas and cultural practices. Asking questions that elicited deeper meanings was another characteristic of this intervention. For example pupils were asked the reasons why they should be open to new dishes: reasons given were its good to try foreign dishes; you must make an effort to try different food; you don't know what it's like unless you try it.

Another intervention in the food and drink topic included short discussion about the symbolism of bread, as well as its nutritional value. In response in a test a number of pupils made a connection between the religious significance of bread with the Christian tradition.

c) *Wider issues relating to French interventions*

The other issues which arose through values interventions was the 'lived' nature of the values in the classroom and the school. For example discussions were held about lying, trusting others and respecting others in the context of learning. Here the teacher consciously engaged with pupils in the application of the school's values to life in school.

The introduction of this approach in year ten meant that the pupils' vocabulary skills had not been developed to cover this type of conversation during key stage three, and thus the lack of language skills impeded the values conversations in the target language and indeed the language development itself. However if this approach were to be included from year seven this problem would be addressed, as would the issue of time and space within the schemes of work, which is always at a premium.

Another key issue, which arose in the French interventions, was whether or not the introduction of the values teaching should be implicit and informal or explicit and named as such. For year 10 in French the solution of filtering the values into the content and process of French teaching was chosen because it still used the language of the values, but allowed the issues to arise naturally, thus not appearing to be intrusive to potentially sceptical year 10 pupils. Once the pupils had grasped the relevance of the values they were then developed more formally.

7. Religious Education

Religious Education lessons were conducted with a mixed ability year 10 GCSE class. The attainment of pupils in both target and control groups therefore reflected the middle ability band at the school. Pupils were monitored in Religious Education from year 7 and an assessment of their results made for sets that began in year 10. A variety of pupils were selected for the research. Issues such as social class, gender, ethnic origins were considered before selection was made therefore registers of groups were checked and the free school lunch menu was examined in order that the sample of pupils represented far as possible the most holistic view of pupils attending the school.

d) *Stages from birth to death: Value focus: God not God (Faith in Christ)*

Initially the aim of the lesson was to explore the notion of commitment and examine how the theme relates to stages in humankind's "Journey through Life". The religious element of the journey was to be considered following pupils' first response. Each individual thought about their personal journey using a relevant worksheet. Pupils had previously examined the concept of commitment and their job was to consider each stage in relation to their suggested stages. For example, becoming a sports teacher required a commitment to keeping fit or going to University required a commitment to study hard.

The aim of the lesson in view of the values intervention was to then introduce explicitly Christian rites of passage and examine how commitment via faith was a pre requisite. However the lesson's aim developed in itself as several pupils included baptism and marriage in church as important stages in their own imaginary life's journey. This was a clear illustration of the consensus on the schools value "Faith in Christ'. Pupils were proud to share their ideas and others listened thoughtfully. Christian rites were introduced as planned following this and pupils discussed maturely how each related to the notion of commitment. A pupil comment that was noted in the logbook was "These stages in life show people you really believe in God". The general feeling of the class shown later in written work was that people must be committed to their faith before embarking on each stage, as each one reaffirmed belief in God.

e) *Baptism Past and Present: Value Focus: Being Fair/Unfair (Justice)*

To begin the topic of baptism the teacher highlighted how society today takes baptism as a rite in which Christians partake. The group had briefly explored persecution of Christians during the ages as part of their previous module. The aim of the lesson was to contrast the ways in which society (past and present) treated believing Christians who wanted to be baptised. We talked about fair treatment of people in society by means of what it meant to be a free thinking/acting citizen. Pupils discussed sensibly their beliefs on the rights of individuals. Amongst the ideas discussed were whether people should have the right to practise a religious belief. It was decided this was right if its conditions were "acceptable to a tolerant society". The teacher then read a story about a Christian family who were committed to the faith and decided to become baptised in the years after Jesus' death. They knew of the risks facing them. The story ended sadly and consequently the whole family was sentenced to death.

A discussion followed about this scenario and clearly pupils understood the issue of justice in relation to the event. Introducing a topic through a story was extremely effective. By explicitly linking in the value of justice it was necessary to begin the section of work in a different way from normal. The intervention helped pupils think more carefully about the nature of baptism, pupils began to feel and understand how committed early Christians were to their faith. The group ·recognised how unjust society was for early Christians but also the dedication and strength of the people to carry out what they believed was good and right.

In many respects teaching in Religious Education is already value laden in relation to ethics and spirituality and there was therefore less difference for pupils and teachers between the experience of teaching and learning with the target group and the control groups.

8. Geography

The target class was a year seven group, taught as a mixed ability tutor group. In reality they were above average ability. Values interventions were introduced in the themes of settlement, the case study of Bristol, the evolution and significance of transport and understanding the shape of the earth.

a) Road Planning

The first target lesson consisted of a role-play of a public enquiry debating whether to allow a new road by-pass to the town of Nailsea. Resources used were all in the textbook and the work relied heavily on an understanding of previous map work. The values targeted were stewardship and respecting others. Pupils were prepared and each pupil had a role that they had to represent at the enquiry. The previous lesson and homework were used to write speeches in preparation.

The classroom was rearranged to simulate a public meeting in a village hall. The teacher was the inspector and admitted pupils 'in role' with a few excursions out of role to register and remind them of purpose. The values targeted were explicitly discussed and written on the board as a reminder. Pupils were reminded prior to the lesson that in looking at changing the environment we have a duty of care to understand the impact and effects of a change such as a new road and that this would be discussed in depth in the public meeting. In such a meeting people would be expected to listen carefully and with respect to others, whether or not their views were shared. Each speaker was allowed to take two questions. The lesson was also recorded on video camera.

Issues of stewardship were very well covered with farmers not wanting to change land use, noise and safety and destruction of habitats being discussed animatedly. There were several occasions particularly towards the end of the lesson when the class was reminded, when being partisan, of the focus on respect. At the end there was a vote. A few minutes were spent at the end of the lesson reviewing how well the class had understood and utilised the school's values, particularly the issues of stewardship.

b) Geography - Shape of the Earth

Later in the year the class was looking at the shape of the earth and our understanding of this as an introduction to longitude and latitude. The first lesson consisted of a question and answer warm up, responding to the question 'What is the shape of the earth?' 'Where is the earth in space?' and 'how do we know?', This was followed by a 10 to 15 minute story of western understanding of the earth's shape and position in the universe. Key dates and the teacher wrote up key dates, words or phrases in a time-line as the story progressed.

The stages were:

- The Bible, Genesis chap.1, 'The Creation'. Earth at the centre of the universe.
- 150 AD Ptolemy & the 'Flat Earth' ideas.
- 1534 Nicholas Copernicus, theory of earth as a rotating planet.
- 1632 AD Galileo's publication of his mathematical proof
- 1665 AD Sir Isaac Newton's discovery of gravity 7 its explanation of the revolution of planets in a solar system.
- Today: Space exploration. Telescopes and rapid communication. Most people accept unquestioningly the earth as a spherical planet in a bigger universe.

After the story of the gradual understanding a short discussion took place, questioning and clarifying the events and why, particularly, Galileo was punished for explaining his mathematical theories and at the same time accepting the church and God.

Pupils wrote their own summary of the storyline in their books. The class then reflected together on what it was like for Galileo as on old, ill, isolated man going blind in prison. How would he describe what had happened to him and what would he feel about it? How would he feel toward the church and God?

Individually and in silence pupils wrote down their own reflections, some of which were then read aloud to the class. Everyone who offered to read had written that they felt it was unfair, they blamed the inquisition but that they would still believe in God. Pupils had great enthusiasm for reading out their thoughts and no concern or embarrassment at declaring a continued belief in God. The one Muslim in the class had written the same view about attitude to God. When the teacher asked if anyone had written that they would stop believing in God as a result, there was unanimous agreement that they would not. Perhaps because they are year seven and in a secure environment in a Church school with regular worship this was wholly acceptable to them. By this time the pupils had had several interventions and they were used to looking at values in geography lessons. This might have helped them to express their ideas more readily. The teacher told the pupils at the end of the lesson that the church had apologised in 1984.

c)   *Geography - Fieldwork*

Other particularly successful interventions took place with geography fieldwork when the value of trust became a focus. It was easy for the class to see the importance of their being trustworthy in behaviour and with belongings. Expectations were made clear and the fact that they were being trusted on a ·boat trip and walkabout. The class wrote down the importance of trust in this situation. Some of their responses explored areas that the teacher had not considered, one example of many stated "Yes, I did trust others, because I trusted the boat driver to take us down the river and back safely. I also trusted my teacher to look after me".

d) Geography - Evaluation

There was a lot of verbal discussion when looking at the theme of forgiveness in relation to the rebuilding of Bristol's City centre as a result of bomb damage. This was centred on an activity interpreting photographs and written and verbal anecdotes. In addition the involvement of Bristol in the slave trade as an area requiring forgiveness was brought up. Some very perceptive comments were expressed, noting the need to be forgiven for some actions, to forgive for others and the importance of forgiveness to enable us to move forward in life. At the same time there was a small contingent of a few boys who wanted to express anti – German feeling and were not easily prepared to look at forgiveness seriously.

Within this subject many of the school's values are integral to an appreciation of the location and interaction of people in places. Explaining specific values has, for the most part, added an extra dimension to lessons on a spiritual, reflective level and has also led to a build up of trust and respect as these reflections have been shared. It has frequently put an extra expectation and responsibility on pupils and serves as a reminder to them of their role and influence in their own development. In addition it has added meaning outside the search for 'pure' subject specific knowledge and skills and has opened out topics in a wider social, and often global, context.

9. Music

The Music National Curriculum orders place emphasis on Music as a practical and creative subject. There are four Attainment Targets: Composing, Performing, Listening and Appraising within which teachers are allowed freedom to follow their own interests, for example choosing their own examples. The experimental class was a Year Nine mixed ability class.

a) *Music - End of unit assessment – valuing ourselves and others*

The objectives of the lesson were

i)   To develop Listening and Appraising skills
ii)   To comment on and grade practical work.

In this lesson the stated aims were achieved by combining them so that the class listened to each others work (produced in groups of four or five), commented on it and, in discussion with the teacher and the group concerned, arrived at a grade.

The class listened to one of the groups piece and wrote brief comments on it under the headings 'Composing' and 'Performing'. The group whose work had been heard was then invited to feedback on their own thoughts on hearing the piece as a listener, from the 'outside', for the first time. Other members of the class were then invited to comment on the piece and discussion followed (for example on the validity of using a 'sample' or on the appropriateness of the tempo or scoring). The class was then invited to record their own grade for the piece after which the teacher gave a grade with a verbal justification that was open to close scrutiny and vigorous comment.

Music Teachers will recognise this lesson as corresponding to current thinking on assessment in the Music classroom and many school Music Departments follow similar procedures. Such lessons also afford an opportunity for significant values related issues to be raised, in fact they cannot be avoided particularly during discussion.

Listening focuses attention on the need to respect others and on the validity of diverse responses to a given stimulus. Discussing also focuses on variety of response. Through encouraging all pupils to contribute and ensuring that they are allowed to, and through accepting and giving only positively expressed comments self-esteem is raised and pupils valuing of themselves reinforced.

In giving grades pupils were allowed the possibility of discriminating between members of each group and the issue of the individuals relationship to a community, potential and justice were raised. Because of the subjective nature of much of the marking criteria, issues of the nature of 'truth' become prominent. As all pupils took part in the same process a degree of relating to one another took place that went beyond sympathy to empathy.

The written notes made by the class in no way express the richness of the verbal exchanges made by the class.

It will be noted that in this lesson it is the *process* of the lesson itself that forms the central content of the lesson. This concentration on 'process' is an important feature of music as a classroom subject. In appraising and composing, what is said i.e. the content is individual and cannot be taught. Rather it is the processes of appraising and of composing which can. Because of this emphasis on process values in music are more readily evident in pedagogy and application than intrinsic to the content of the lesson.

b) Music - Group Work

Another values intervention in music related to processes of time management and group work. A teacher led question and answer session led to ideas and examples of good time management being written on the board. Pupils were then asked to brainstorm ideas on what they thought a group of people needed to do in order to work well together, themselves working in mixed gender groups with people they had not worked with previously. An end time for each group to report their findings to the rest of the class was given. In order to complete this task successfully the pupils had to demonstrate good time management and group work skills so that the process and content of the lesson were synonymous.

All groups concluded that it was important to value everyone equally and to be fair, and came up with examples of things needing to be done to achieve this, such as being positive in commenting on each others ideas. There were obvious connections between these ideas and those inherent in the 'Listening and Appraising' process.

Focusing on these skills, which pupils are asked to use in most practical music lessons, turned out to have a continuing benefit in the way in which pupils worked in subsequent lessons. They had point of reference, of good practice, to refer back to. Their levels of skill and understanding were raised in a fundamental area that enabled them to work more productively.

This practical outcome was very important because it was very evident to the pupils and clearly represented the school's values in practice. It was also clear that values might be used as a tool that can facilitate the transfer of learning from classroom theory to lived practice.

10. Second Year Interventions

During the next academic year this first group of teachers continued to develop values interventions with the same year groups, and to share the practice and strategies with their departments. In addition, further experimental values interventions were devised in the subjects of history, design technology, maths and science. The purpose of this year's work was to further understand the nature of the teaching and learning processes which occur during the interventions and to explore any effects on specific learning outcomes within the subject.

The outcomes of both years' work are set out in the following chapter.

Chapter Seven
Discussion of Findings

1. Discussion of Findings: Repertory Grid Analysis

The analysis of the Repertory Grid data took the following form. With the first tranche of grids (data 1) the Ingrid and Series programmes were used to elicit the basic information about each individual and each of ten groups - five target groups and five control groups by subject. This initial analysis showed that the values as constructs were meaningful to the pupils, and that each of the elements selected fell within the range of convenience for those constructs - in other words each of the school's values was relevant to the subjects being studied. The rating of the constructs was generally towards the positive pole (i.e. being fair) of the constructs rather than the negative pole (being unfair) and there was a range of scores of 4, which was designated as 'neither pole matters'. No further analysis was undertaken at this point.

After the second tranche of Repertory Grids was elicited from the pupils it was possible to analyse the data from a number of perspectives. Four individual's data was deemed 'null', one because the pupil did not fill in the questionnaire properly and three because of absences.

2. Analysis of Data

The first stage of analysis was to draw up a basic table for each of the target and control pupils using INGRID and DELTA output. An example is shown is below. The mean of each pupil's rating score on each construct (1-9) was calculated for the first and second grid (M1 and M2) and the difference between them. The same was done for the variation around the mean for each construct for the first and second grid (V1 and V2), and for the variation as a percentage of the whole

(AS%1 and AS%2). The figures for the variation as a ratio
were available but these were not used.

Data 1

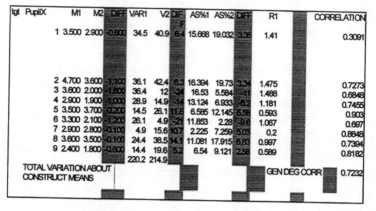

tgt PupilX	M1	M2	DIFF	VAR1	V2 DIF F	AS%1	AS%2	DIFF	R1	CORRELATION
1	3.500	2.900	-0.600	34.5	40.9 6.4	15.668	19.032	3.36	1.41	0.3091
2	4.700	3.600	-1.100	36.1	42.4 6.3	16.394	19.73	3.34	1.475	0.7273
3	3.600	2.000	-1.600	36.4	12 -24	16.53	5.584	-11	1.488	0.6848
4	2.900	1.900	-1.000	28.9	14.9 -14	13.124	6.933	-6.2	1.181	0.7455
5	3.500	3.700	0.200	14.5	26.1 11.6	6.585	12.145	5.56	0.593	0.903
6	3.300	2.100	-1.200	26.1	4.9 -21	11.853	2.28	-9.6	1.067	0.697
7	2.900	2.800	-0.100	4.9	15.6 10.7	2.225	7.259	5.03	0.2	0.8848
8	3.600	3.500	-0.100	24.4	38.5 14.1	11.081	17.915	6.83	0.997	0.7394
9	2.400	1.800	-0.600	14.4	19.6 5.2	6.54	9.121	2.58	0.589	0.8182
				220.2	214.9					
TOTAL VARIATION ABOUT CONSTRUCT MEANS								GEN DEG CORR		0.7232

Finally the first and second grids were put through the DELTA
program which gave a correlation statistic that measured the
degree of correlation between the first and second grid by each
of the nine constructs, and a general degree of correlation for
the whole grids. This basic data then enabled the sample to be
examined by groups of control and target pupils as a whole,
and as subgroups according to subject.

2. School Values as Constructs

The constructs, drawn from the school's core values, were
numbered as follows:

	School Value	Core Value as Construct
1	Truth	Being truthful - not being truthful
2	Stewardship	Taking care of people & things - not taking care of people & things
3	Forgiveness	Forgiving - not forgiving
4	Justice	Being fair - not being fair
5	Faith in Christ	God - not God
6	Fulfilling our Potential	Doing my best - not doing my best
7	Trustworthiness	Trusting and being trusted - Not trusting and being trusted
8	Valuing ourselves	Respecting myself - not respecting myself
9	Valuing others	Respecting other people - not respecting other people

3. Pupil X: Science and Truthfulness

In this example the pupil shows some distinct changes in the mean score per construct for most of the constructs. The pupil was a member of the target sample for Science in year eight. What can be understood from this grid is that after the teaching and learning interventions her average rating on construct one changed from a mean of 3.5 which meant that in her perception truth was not very closely connected to science to a mean of 2.9 which meant that her perception after the teaching and learning interventions was that being truthful was more closely connected to science. The variation around the mean increased from 15.6% on the first grid to 19.032% on the second grid.

The degree of correlation between her ratings on 'being truthful' before and after the teaching and learning interventions was 0.3091. Given that a correlation score of 1 means that there is no difference between the two, this score indicates quite a large degree of change on this construct.

It is possible to assert that for this pupil her use of the construct of truthfulness - untruthfulness had increased, and that the direction of that change was towards the value of truthfulness, rather than untruthfulness or the irrelevance of truthfulness to science. If truthfulness can be understood as a core value, which has spiritual, moral, social and cultural aspects to it, and if changes in the use of that core value can be construed as an intended 'development' then it can be argued that spiritual, moral, social and cultural development has taken place. To understand whether that 'development' was likely to have been spiritual, moral, social or cultural one would have to examine the processes of teaching and learning which were taking place during the interventions. An examination of the qualitative findings of the research has an explanatory role at this point. Two of the agreed outcomes from the teacher researchers, including Science, were that

➢ Values interventions add a spiritual dimension to lessons because they encourage a reflective searching for deeper meaning to events and issues.

➢ Values interventions appear to encourage pupil responsiveness. This may be because they engage the whole child as a learner, including their emotions, their spirituality and their sense of activism.

t	pupilY	M1	M2	Dif	V1	V2	Dif	As%1	As%2	Dif	Ratio	Ratio	Correlation
1		2.400	1.500	-0.900	14.4	8.5	-5.9	10.596	11.565	0.97	0.954	1.041	0.8848
2		3.700	1.700	-2.000	28.1	4.1	-24	20.677	5.578	-15.1	1.861	0.502	0.5879
3		3.100	2.500	-0.600	10.9	10.5	-0.4	8.021	14.286	6.27	0.722	1.286	0.9273
4		2.300	2.100	-0.200	10.1	6.9	-3.2	7.432	9.388	1.96	0.669	0.845	0.9758
5		4.300	4.300	0.000	8.1	10.1	2	5.96	13.741	7.78	0.536	1.237	0.8788
6		2.900	1.900	-1.000	20.9	12.9	-8	15.379	17.551	2.17	1.384	1.58	0.8909
7		2.400	2.000	-0.400	20.4	6	-14.4	15.011	8.163	-6.85	1.351	0.735	0.9152
8		2.900	2.400	-0.500	12.9	10.4	-2.5	9.492	14.15	4.66	0.854	1.273	0.8485
9		2.300	1.700	-0.600	10.1	4.1	-6	7.432	5.578	-1.85	0.669	0.502	0.8667
	TOTAL VARIATION ABOUT CONSTRUCT MEANS				135.9	73.5					**GEN DEG CORR**		0.864

4. Pupil Y: French and Valuing Others

Another example is Pupil X, a year ten French student from the target group. Her basic data is shown in the table below:

From this data it can be seen that the mean for Pupil Y's rating of the construct of valuing others has changed from 2.3 to 1.7. This indicates that in her perception the core value of respecting others has become more closely connected to aspects of her French learning after the interventions than before. The variation around the mean of that construct has actually reduced for the second grid. This can indicate that she is actually using the construct in a less discriminating way in fact she is using it less. However since a score of 1 indicates the quality of 'goodness' on this grid it could mean that she is more definite in her mind about the relevance of 'valuing others' in her understanding of French. The correlation ·between the ratings of the two constructs on the two occasions is 0.8667, which means that there is a difference between the two scores.

Overall, the mean scores of the constructs have moved towards the emergent pole of the construct (towards a score of 1) apart from the construct of God and not God. This indicates that she continues to see the construct of God as not very relevant to learning French although a change in the variation around the mean from 5.96% to 13.741% indicates that she is actually using the construct with more discrimination after the teaching and learning interventions.

5. Significance of Findings

The data on each pupil and on each group of pupils by subject is interesting, and can be seen to be consistent with the qualitative findings of the study. It offers profitable ways of understanding and explaining what has been happening with each pupil during the five sets of teaching and learning interventions. However it is important to look at the data as a whole in order to see what the overall patterns are and whether there are any statistically significant changes.

6. Control and Target Pupils from the Whole Population: Average Scores

The following tables show the Average means per construct before and after the teaching and learning interventions for 23 target pupils and 23 control pupils. These are means of means, and by definition the score becomes more averaged out, and less extreme.

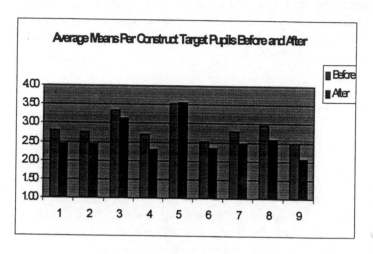

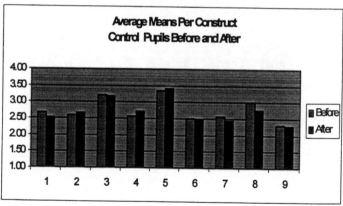

From these tables it can be seen that there is more change towards the emergent pole of the constructs (the rating of 1, or the 'goodness' end of the values) amongst the target population as a whole than there is in the control population as a whole. However, to get some statistical indication whether there is reason to believe that this change could be due to the teaching and learning interventions or to chance, it was necessary to undertake further tests.

7. Control and Target Pupils: Correlations

The General Correlation figures (a measure of sameness and difference) for the before and after grids of 23 Target and 23 Control pupils was also subject to a T Test to discover the likelihood of the changes between the two groups being due chance or to some other factor. The T Test applied to the control and target figures returned a probability of 0.13 that the two samples came from the same population. In other words there is a 13% likelihood that the two groups come from the same population and that the differences between them are random. Whilst this figure is low, it is not statistically significant. Tables showing the general correlation figures are presented in two forms below, the first in alphabetical order of pupils in the group, the second in ascending order of correlation within each group.

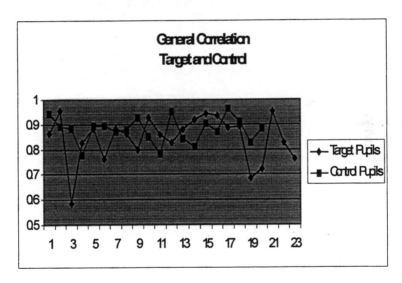

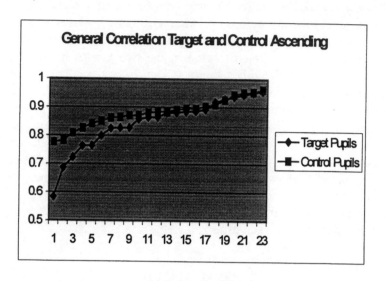

8. Looking at the Whole Population in terms of each Construct

A detailed examination of the data by each construct revealed more sensitive information, which enabled the researchers to make judgements about the ways in which the control and target groups of the population used each value as construct before and after the teaching and learning interventions. This data can be displayed in various formats, including lists of mean scores for each construct by target and control group. A useful way of presenting the changes between the target and control pupils before and after the teaching and learning interventions for each construct is shown in the table below. The chart shows the amount and direction of change in the mean score by pupil in the target and control groups for the construct of being fair /being unfair. Changes above 0 refer to changes towards the contrast pole of the construct i.e. being unfair, whereas changes below 0 refer to changes towards the emergent pole of the construct i.e. being fair.

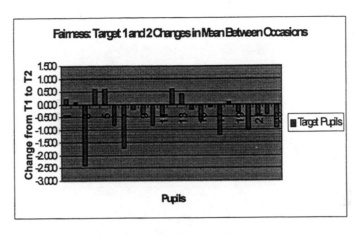

The information gained from this analysis was set into four groups of average means per construct for Target and Control Groups. The two-tailed T test was selected as a simple test that is able to analyse two arrays of data to give a percentage probability of the two samples coming from the same population. For this analysis the mean scores per pupil for each construct were calculated and allocated into four sets - Target Pupils before the interventions (T1), Control Pupils before the interventions (C1); Target Pupils after the interventions (T2) and Control Pupils after the interventions (C2). Scores for each of the nine constructs were thus available in four combinations and were subjected to a two-tailed T Test. The results of the T Tests are set out in the table below:

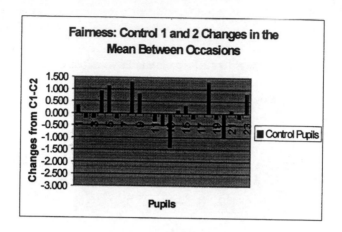

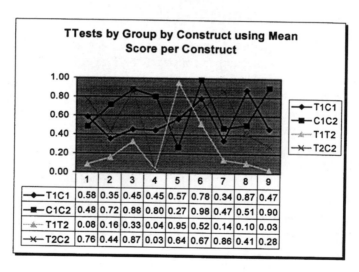

	1	2	3	4	5	6	7	8	9
T1C1	0.58	0.35	0.45	0.45	0.57	0.78	0.34	0.87	0.47
C1C2	0.48	0.72	0.88	0.80	0.27	0.98	0.47	0.51	0.90
T1T2	0.08	0.16	0.33	0.04	0.95	0.52	0.14	0.10	0.03
T2C2	0.76	0.44	0.87	0.03	0.64	0.67	0.86	0.41	0.28

From these tests, the statistically significant results are found in the combination of the Target pupils before the teaching and learning interventions and the Target Pupils after the teaching and learning interventions (T1 T2, C1 C2). This is an expected result. The T Tests indicated that Target Pupils before the interventions and the Control Pupils before the interventions were very likely to have been the same population and the Control Pupils before the interventions and the Control Pupils after the interventions were also very likely to have been the same population. An apparent anomaly was found in the results of the T Test of the Target Pupils and Control Pupils after the interventions. Here the results indicated that it was likely that the two groups did, on eight out of ten constructs, come from the same population - in fact the expectation would have been that they should be different. However on examination of the figures it became clear that relative to their starting scores, the control group had remained broadly the same over the two occasions. However the Target Group had in fact changed in a direction which firstly moved towards the Control Group, then crossed over it and moved away, but resulting in a position which was still apparently deemed by the T Test to be within the same population.

A probability score on the T Test of 0.05, taking into account the degrees of freedom indicated by the size of the sample, was deemed to indicate some significance. A five- percent chance of the two groups coming from the same population indicates that it is likely that some thing other than chance will account for the differences. The two constructs which scored at this level on the test (T1 and T2) were Valuing Others and Fairness, with Truth coming very close with a score of 0.08.

The constructs of God - not God and doing my best -not doing my best scored the lowest, with the high probability that the two samples came from the same population. All of the other constructs scored with a low probability, though they did not have statistical significance.

From this data it can be seen that there have been changes in the ways in which the target pupils used the core values as constructs after the teaching and learning interventions which were greater than changes in the control groups. These were often changes in mean score towards the 'goodness' end of the construct, and also changes in the amount of discrimination in the ways the constructs were used in relation to the elements. Some of these changes are statistically significant.

It can therefore be argued that planned teaching and learning interventions in the taught curriculum which promote core values which are intrinsic to the subject and to the teaching methodology can lead to changes in the ways pupils construe those core values in relation to the subject. To the extent that increased thinking about, and increased quality of the perceived relationship between 'justice' and 'geography' can be argued to entail spiritual, moral, social and cultural aspects and processes, then these changes can be seen as spiritual, moral, social and cultural development of pupils within the curriculum.

9. The relationship between interventions and changes in repertory grid data.

a) Science:

During the interventions all of the values were visited to some degree, although some were visited more regularly or more effectively than others.   Those that were dealt with most effectively or regularly were; being truthful, respecting myself, respecting others, and being fair.   The value that was addressed least was faith in Christ.

Six of the nine values showed a decrease in mean score for the target pupils, alongside an increase, or no change in the mean score for the control pupils.
These were truthfulness, taking care of other people/things, being fair, trusting and being trusted, respecting myself, and respecting others.   A decrease in the mean score for a value indicates that the pupils perceive there to be a stronger connection between the value and science after the interventions compared with before the interventions.   The values that showed such a decrease included all the values that had been given the strongest emphasis during the interventions.

Five of the nine values showed an increase in variation for the target pupils, indicating that pupils were giving more thought to the way that they connected these values with science.

These five were; being truthful, being fair, doing my best, trusting and being trusted, and respecting others. However, two of these, being truthful and trusting/ being trusted, also increased in the control group.

Overall, the four values that showed the greatest change were; being truthful, being fair, trusting/being trusted and respecting others. Three of these correspond to values that were most strongly targeted during interventions, while trusting/being trusted altered despite only limited intervention. Respecting myself, which was strongly targeted, showed only limited changes.

b) Music:

The analysis of the mean scores of the constructs for the target and control pupils in the Music sample indicated an increased awareness of all the constructs in both the control and target groups, with the exception of a very slight variance in the case of the control groups understanding of 'God'. In the case of all the constructs except 'trust' and 'self-respect' there is a significantly greater increase in the target groups awareness of the constructs when compared to the control group.

Analysis of the use of each construct shows that there is a falling off in the use of each value, except that of 'respecting myself', in the control group. In the target group use of 'being truthful', 'taking care of people and things', 'being fair', 'trusting and being trusted' and 'respecting myself' increased.

Comparison of two identical twins, one in the target and one in the control group is revealing. In all cases the target twin shows a significantly greater awareness of the constructs except for a drift away from the construct 'God' which is mirrored by both girls.

Some constructs, which had been emphasised over the year, appear to be more used by the target pupils than those which had featured less prominently, for example 'taking care of people and things', 'being fair' and 'trusting and being trusted' compared with 'God' and 'forgiving'.

c) Geography:

In the geography group the analysis of the Repertory Grid data showed an increased use of the constructs of doing one's best, trust, self respect and respecting others, God and forgiveness in the target group. Use of some of these was also raised in the control group, but here there was an increased connection between the values of respect for one's self and others, doing one's best and trust, but a decrease in connecting God and forgiveness with equivalent aspects of the curriculum. Both target and control groups seemed to show less connection of use of truth, forgiveness and stewardship with the subject.

In the early part of the year the class had interventions which focussed more on the content of the geography curriculum, covering the values of stewardship, fairness, forgiveness and respecting others. Truthfulness was covered in one lesson at the same time as covering aspects of belief in God and was much less explicitly looked at than most other values.

The general shift toward relating taught elements of geography with the values of respecting one's self and others, trust and doing one's best were emphasised more frequently and concentrated in the latter part of the year, closer to the second data collection. This took place within a topic looking at the growth of Bristol and included fieldwork, group work, and presentations. Several opportunities were taken to review the impact of individual behaviour on others and this seems to have had some more influence on the pupil relation of the ·school values to their lessons than the earlier work which was more specifically content related.

The results showed a general shift, although the extent of the differences measured on the five target pupils was not as great as might have been expected from the responses in class. There was also a more significant shift in the use of constructs of trust and self-respect in the control group than was seen in the target group, although both the target and the control group were making strong connections with these values and the curriculum in the first questionnaire.

d) Religious Education:

Trusting and Truth

The values of trust and truth were incorporated into a number of lessons on marriage. The lessons had a number of themes one of which drew upon the symbolism of the ring and another practicalities of marriage in the 1990's. The results show the target group recognised the significance of trust in marriage more than the control, in addition the control groups opinion on its significance remained static.

Justice

A similar pattern emerged in relation to justice. A shift in emphasis occurred, thus pupils in the target group recognised more readily the significance of justice. Lessons, which included themes of justice, related to baptism (infant vs. believers), death, marriage, divorce and those incorporating group work.

Negative Scores

Faith in Christ proved to have a more negative mean score in the target group. A number of explanations for this are possible. In the target group there were focused and heated discussions about the existence of God. Experience of .sensitive issues relating to marriage, divorce and death can also leave pupils feeling vulnerable at a time when many of them are actively questioning religious belief. However the variation about the mean was greater in the target group which indicated that these pupils were using the construct with more discrimination than the control group, considering its implications and making value judgements accordingly.

e) *French:*

Valuing ourselves and valuing others were the focus in the topic on food. The initial relation to the idea of "foreign" food was quite negative and some time was spent on discussing the importance of trying new things and respecting other people's likes and dislikes. "European" menus were drawn up, which included reasons why people should try to learn about other cultures. The graph of the target group shows that the pupils were more aware of these values in the topic of food after having experienced the interventions whereas the control group graph shows little or no change.

The value focus for the work on "Creating your own environment" was 'stewardship'. Here the pupils were given free rein to decide on the needs of a new community. The graph of the target group for the value of stewardship shows not only a positive mean shift from before and after the intervention, but also a much greater shift compared to the results of the control group graph. The interventions were very easy to introduce into this topic.

There are also small changes in the values of forgiveness and justice in the before and after results of the target group. There are also significant changes when compared to the results of these values in the control group. The changes here may be due to the fact that some time was spent on the idea of "forgiveness" and "being fair", not only in the element "Creating a new community" but also in the element "Making a complaint in a shop". Although these values were not discussed for any length of time, they were introduced as "undercurrents" into a dialogue in French taking place in a shop. It does seem however, that they still had an effect on the final results.

Examples of Pupils Work

11.2.99   <u>Charles Drew: 'The Unexpugated version</u>
H/W

The meaning of the word:
Unexpurgated. 'Unclean, unpurified and unclean.

Ghetto: Slum area where the deprived minority live.

No my views on Charles Drew haven't changed as I still think he was good at sport and was really clever.

After reading the passage I felt sad and really upset how people treated black people because of their skin. I also think that it was nasty how people used Charles's techniches but because he was black they wouldn't treat him and because of that he died. I felt happy for him though because he discovered one of the best things in medical history and I also felt angry.

1.2.99   <u>CHARLE DREW: THE UNEXPUGATED</u>
              <u>VERSION</u>
H/W

1.   Meanings:
       UNEXPURGATED means unclean

       GHETTO means a slum area which the
       deprived minority live

2)   *No, I still think he was a very clever man and
       go at sport but now I think he was very
       deterrmined to succseed because of his colour*

3)   I feel that

       -   *Quite sad because he died because the
           hospital would'nt take him because of he
           was coloured*
       -   Happy because he inveted something that
           might save you and me
       -   Angry because the hospital told him to go
           to the black hospital when he was ddieing
       -    Unhappy because the hotel refused to
           serve black people
       -   Upset because of the way he died

LE MENU POUR LE EU

Raison pour aller manger ia.

C'est bien de gouter lees plates etrangers.
C'est important de goute la nourrture des autres pays.
If fait faire un effort de manger la nouriture deffente.

Boissons

Cola
Lemonade
Biere
Vin rouge
Thé
Café

◆

Le entrée menu

Croissant.
C'est une patisserie sucree.

◆

Le principal menu

Paella.
C'est du riz avec des fruits de mer on quelquefois aves du
poulet.

◆

Bacon and eggs
C'est porc et ouef

◆

Piri Piri
C;est du poulet qui vivant, a mange beaucoup de poivre.
Quand on le mange, le poulet a un gout tres piquant

◆

Goulash

13.11.98   Practical work in Music

1)   Time Management

  - work out what needs to be done
  - set yourself short term targets

Eg. Task to compose, notate, rehearse and perform a 'Blues.'

i)   30 mins
  - Getting equipment ÷ 5 mins
  - Brainstorm of ideas ÷ 10 mins
  - Select ideas ÷ 5 mins
  - Develop opening ÷ 5 mins

Practical Work in Music

<u>Working with others</u>

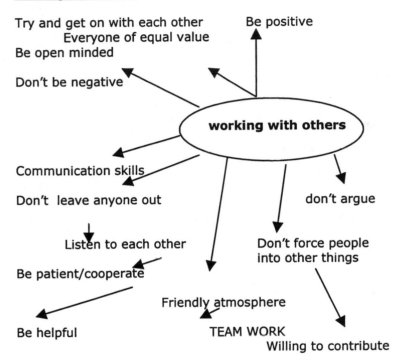

Try and get on with each other
Everyone of equal value
Be open minded

Don't be negative

Be positive

working with others

Communication skills

Don't leave anyone out

don't argue

Listen to each other

Be patient/cooperate

Don't force people
into other things

Friendly atmosphere

Be helpful

TEAM WORK

Willing to contribute

Some Reflections on Values from Year Seven Geography

<u>Trust on The Docks Trip.</u>   <u>20th April.</u>

Did I meet my target?

Yes, I think I did meet my target I followed instructions, I didn't bring extra baggage and I brought a snack and a waterproof coat. I think I was trustworthy because I didn't run off or stand up on the boat, but I do think I could have listened more and payed more attention.

Also I did trust others not to push me off the boat or leave me behind and I trusted the boat driver not to crash or get us hurt and I trusted the teachers to take care of me.

Galileo's life sentence

I have a life sentence! I have only just heard this is the inquistion saying so. I still believe in God, He must have a reason for imprisoning me or He wouldn't have done it. I mean, why else would they have done it? I must speak to my wife, she'll understand and support me in this. I worry now about how it will be ... .but I am sure my theorys right.

Later: It's awful! I hate it! I'm going out of my mind. I am so glad I have pen and paper.

Votre Ville Ideale

Les personnes qui y habitent:
Monsierr Smith - il est fermier, il est fort et semer
Monsierr Rode - il est macon, il est fort et gentil
Madame Luci - elle est institurteur, elle est soigner
Monsierr John Paul - il est pretre, elle est honnete
Monsierr Ben - il est ouvier, il est fort et dilligent
Madame Kate - elle est cuisiner, elle est adroi
Monsierr Chris - il est sodat, il est fort et ter un coup de feu
Monsierr Vert - il est forge, il est dillegent et determine

Les Batiments
Pour les enfants il y a ecole.
Pour les chretiens il y a eglise
Pour les feriers il y a ferme
Pour les malade il y a hopital
Pour les communite, il y a masion
Pour les communite tout le monde, il y a magasin

LES REGLES
On ne doit pas fumer.
On ne doit pas jurer
On doit respecter les gens
On doit respecter le dieu
On ne doit pas voler
On ne doit pas jeter du papier
On ne doit pas tuer
On doit respecter les animoux

AUTRE INFORMATION

Temps il fait du soleil dans en ete, et if fait froid dans uen hiver. Je Le vais encore batir l'hopital et maison de correction. Il fait avoir gare.

Hopital est plus important que maison de correction

Year 10 French

C.1. Mon aimez manger est poulet. [J'aime manger. I want to eat]

2. Mon n'aimez manger est petit pois

3. Mon boisson prefere est a Verre due coca

4. Pour le petit dejeuner je mnge ou pain grille et a verre du jus d'orange

5. Mon repas prefere est piri-piri et frites

6. Mon plat aimeriez-vous gouter est Viande

7. Mon plat prefere parce-que Viande's et gouter

8. Je manger quatre trance du pain chaque jour

9. Oui, je achetes le pain [où? - where?]

10. Oui, le pain significatif parce-que le Jesus (communion)

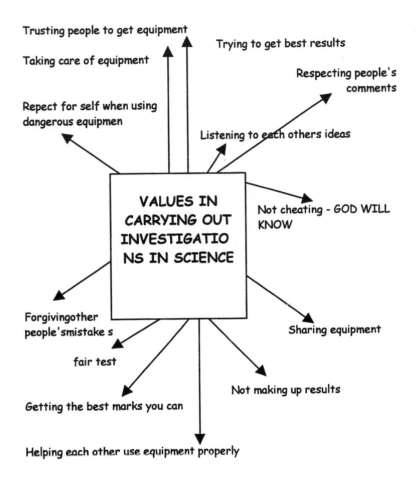

Trusting people to get equipment

Taking care of equipment

Trying to get best results

Respecting people's comments

Repect for self when using dangerous equipmen

Listening to each others ideas

VALUES IN CARRYING OUT INVESTIGATIO NS IN SCIENCE

Not cheating - GOD WILL KNOW

Forgivingother people'smistake s

Sharing equipment

fair test

Getting the best marks you can

Not making up results

Helping each other use equipment properly

Chapter Eight
Discussion of Findings: Teaching and Learning Strategies

Purpose of Values interventions

During years two and three of the research programme while teachers were devising and delivering 'values interventions' regular research cluster meetings provided a structured forum for discussion and feedback. These discussions took the form of comparisons between interventions in different subjects, analysis of pupil work, clarification of key themes as they emerged in the values work, and discussion of key ideas. These research meetings were recorded and fed back to the teachers in written form, who then were able to confirm, alter or develop their findings.

The teachers agreed that values interventions were intended to:

Achieve explicit pupil understanding about the meaning and relevance of the particular value or values in focus.

- Achieve a sense of pupil 'ownership' of the value i.e. an emotional commitment to the value plus an understanding of its relevance.
- Encourage pupils to apply the value in the wider context of their lives – promoting community involvement or 'service learning'.
- Encourage pupils to make connections between values learning and their own experience of life.
- Encourage pupils to make connections between values and wider issues of knowledge and culture.

1. The Value of Dialogue and Discussion

A common theme appearing in all the interventions was the value of discussion and dialogue. It was through talking, or structured discussion, that pupils were able to make connections between the value in focus and the wider world or between the specific value and the pupil's personal experience. The sort of connections which were facilitated by the interventions were those connections in which pupils' own experience was highly relevant and where connections, or cognitive and emotional links, were made between that experience, the 'problems' encountered in the values interventions and the wider application of values in society. Interestingly personal experience, specific values problems and the application of values in culture are all understood in the form of narrative – meaning is carried and made accessible through story, regardless of the discipline in which values are encountered. The following diagram attempts to capture this idea about 'making connections' or the intersection of three stories as a creative place for personal growth and learning within the curriculum.

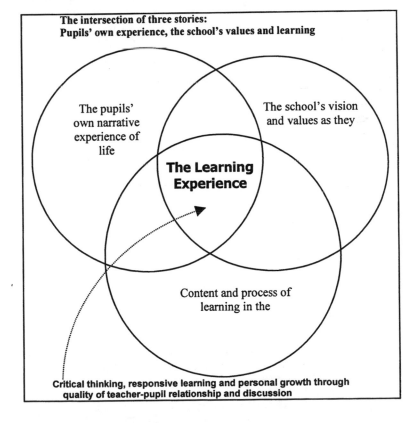

The intersection of three stories:
Pupils' own experience, the school's values and learning

The pupils' own narrative experience of life

The school's vision and values as they

The Learning Experience

Content and process of learning in the

Critical thinking, responsive learning and personal growth through quality of teacher-pupil relationship and discussion

The research team drew upon Hanham's work which suggested that educative discussion moves through three phases – from the descriptive, through to the reflective (asking why) and then through to the speculative (making wider connections, applications and hypotheses). This was seen as a useful tool for structuring the discussions, which occurred either in groups or with the whole class as part of the interventions. Inevitably, values interventions require more than a simple description of a problem. In fact the presentation of a values problem is the starting point from which values work can develop. Values interventions engaged the pupils in reflection – asking why there is a problem, and in speculation about what might be done differently, or how a situation or story might work out differently if other values were brought to bear on the subject. Thus the quality of thinking and talking, and thus learning, in values interventions was of crucial significance to the whole process. Given that that thinking and talking was about those moral and spiritual values which the school community considered to be of ultimate significance, it is possible to argue that quality of language and discourse is also a critical component of spiritual, moral, social and cultural development.

2. Learners as Organised Totalities

This understanding of learning draws upon a view of the learner as an organised totality – a person with a history, a community, hopes, feelings, beliefs, values and attitudes as well as a capacity to learn and to grow. In his book 'Designing and Implementing and Integrated Curriculum' (Clark 1997) argues that thinking and learning are 'integrative, whole-body processes that consist of rational, intuitive, affective, sensory and volitional ways of knowing' and suggests that

> *'intelligence/thinking/learning is a single, dynamic, multi-faceted, functional capacity that is inherent in human consciousness. This capacity may be expressed in a variety of modes'.ibid p29*

Values interventions addressed the whole child as a learner and teacher researchers observed that they related to pupils differently in values intervention lessons. That difference was that they saw the learners as whole people with histories, likes, dislikes and hopes, rather than only as potential scientists, or geographers or musicians. They found values interventions to be a meaningful way of teaching for Personal Social and Health Education, within their normal teaching domain – and this they saw as preferable to taking a 'one off' PSHE slot with a class they did not know, and did not necessarily meet in any other context.

The relevance of Multiple Intelligence Theory to values interventions was evident throughout the research. It offered valuable insights because it suggests that there are ranges of intelligences that can be operative in a learning situation. For personal growth and spiritual and moral development, inter-personal and intra-personal intelligence is as important as linguistic intelligence or logical/mathematical intelligence. Musical, spatial, kinaesthetic and perspectival intelligence are all highly relevant too - acknowledging and affirming a range of intelligences in learners also affirms and acknowledges the learner as a whole person.

The sorts of thinking skills which pupils drew upon in these lessons went beyond those ordinarily utilised in the subject classroom – this was perhaps because the teachers too were thinking differently about learning and teaching. Those thinking skills which were observed throughout the two years of values interventions included creative thinking, systems thinking, critical thinking, speculative thinking as well as 'thinking about thinking' itself. In addition empathy, and emotional intelligence, including self awareness, was stimulated in the context of the interventions.

3. Outcomes

At the end of the two year experimental teaching and learning research phase the teachers spent some time identifying those outcomes which could be validated with evidence from their observations, experience, assessment of pupils and from the Repertory Grid investigations, the questionnaires and interviews. In addition evidence was drawn from pupils' written work - both homework and classwork and these provided a means of comparing and contrasting interventions across the subject area.

These outcomes were categorised into three main groups: Pupil Personal Development, Making Connections and a Holistic Curriculum.

4. Pupil Development

a) There is a strong consensus amongst pupils in this school on the importance of the school's core values.

This was evidenced through discussion and dialogue with pupils in values intervention lessons as well as from the use of the Repertory Grid Questionnaires before and after the interventions. These showed that not only were the core values relevant to pupils, but they tended to rate them towards the positive pole of the rating scale. The core values were identified as a result of a school wide consultation and investigation during the previous year, and the consensus surrounding them provided a sound and justifiable basis for the teaching and learning interventions.

It was possible that through a consultation only, the results might not have enabled the researchers to differentiate between what pupils thought they 'ought' to value and what pupils valued 'in practice', especially in a Church school. However the investigation process and its particular use of Repertory Grid provided some evidence that these were also values which pupils 'actually' believed to be important. In fact, the value about which there was most concern – ie 'faith in Christ' did not appear as a significant value in the consultation process for teachers or pupils. It *did* however, appear as a significant value in the investigation process, although for a small minority of pupils this was not a value that was 'personally held' but was valued because it was perceived to be an integral value of the school community. For another small minority – this value was also strongly associated with the notion of 'freedom of belief' – both freedom to hold a Christian belief and freedom not to.

These core values formed part of the school's vision and provided a frame of reference for the content and process of spiritual, moral, social and cultural development that was envisaged in the school.

The key point is that these values had personal meaning for the pupils and teachers in this particular school and thus they could be utilised and extended as a vehicle for spiritual, moral, social and cultural development. They are key overarching concepts that form part of a broader world-view, or tradition within society and thus they carry with them the possibility of making connections and systems thinking. In other words the school's core values provide a means of enabling pupils to relate differing components of their learning to real life issues – both their own real life experience and those issues which are commonly discussed and 'problematised' in the public square. They provide a vehicle that can enable pupils to make sense and meaning out of their learning.

b) There is, however, often a gap between pupils' espoused values and those in practice.

There was a noticeable gap between what pupils thought and felt was important in terms of values and the behaviour and attitudes which they exhibited at times. This was considered by the teacher researchers to be part of the human condition and underlined the importance of dialogue and vision. Many of the values interventions, almost by definition, explored critical problems associated with values – such as the presence of apparent in-justice, or the outcomes of poor stewardship, or the disrespect of persons. All too often the gap between desired and practiced values is given as a reason not to promote 'idealised' values of the 'apple pie and motherhood variety'. However this is precisely the terrain on which spiritual, moral, social and cultural development *can* take place, both in terms of the self in relation to the self, to others and to the community's vision. It is precisely because there is a gap between what individuals, communities and societies aspire to in terms of ideals and what actually happens in practice, that spiritual, moral, social and cultural development and citizenship is a requirement of education in the first place. It is because humanbeings have the capacity both for great acts of humanitarianism and gross acts of ethnic cleansing that the spiritual, moral, social and cultural direction of education is so important. Hitler's death camps were inevitably 'manned' by highly educated people – knowledge and understanding alone does not make human beings wise, nor does it promote civilisation.

The school's vision and core moral and spiritual values provide an overarching sense of direction for education and learning, which is important. It begins to answer the question of 'education for what?'

c) After two terms of values interventions pupil's moral and spiritual vocabulary had increased and they were more readily able to express their thoughts in this dimension.

This was evident both through teacher observation of the values interventions and through semi-structured interviews with the target and control pupils in year seven. The focus on dialogue during the interventions included the introduction of new language skills and concepts, and pupils were frequently required to articulate their ideas and views relating to the core values. One observation from the first year's consultation was that, even with the 'A' level sociology students who took part in the consultation programme, there was a relatively poor level of discourse about values issues which required attention before those students could then take part in the programme of consulting others.

This issue was brought into stark focus in the values work undertaken in year ten French lessons where the pupils' vocabulary in the target language was largely utilitarian and descriptive. Introducing values issues required learning new vocabulary, although if this issue was addressed in year seven then the range of vocabulary available to pupils by year ten would be different.

The point is that without adequate language we cannot name, discuss and debate our experience as human beings. There is little that is so dis-empowering as having experiences that cannot even be named, let alone spoken of. The Eskimos have many different words for snow – their experience of snow is greater, more pervasive and meaningful than most of the rest of the world, and their language has developed accordingly. Words have power – by not equipping young learners with the words and concepts with which to name and develop the spiritual and moral dimensions of life we do them a great disservice. The importance of quality discourse in this area cannot be under-estimated.

d) Values interventions appear to encourage pupil responsiveness. This may be because they engage the whole child as a learner, including their emotions, their spirituality and their sense of activism and involvement in the community.

·An observation made frequently by the teacher researchers was to do with the level of emotional engagement of pupils with their learning in values interventions lessons. Pupils frequently responded with their own value judgements to issues of injustice, or stewardship or the need to value others and they described personal feelings and responses to their learning.

It was often appropriate, though not often followed up, to develop the intervention into some form of active response - such as writing to the Euro MP, or some other form of community involvement which built upon the pupils engagement with the issues. When pupils expressed anger at injustice, or empathy with those who suffer, they tapped into an energy that could be constructively channelled into action. For example, on a year nine geography project on Brazil, students were emotionally engaged with the suffering of street children of their own age, and impressed by various efforts on the part of charitable organisations to alleviate that suffering. The project included debates with 'Brazilian politicians' from the 6th form about the appropriateness of government strategies to address these problems. As a result of their learning the year nine pupils made a significant contribution to a Traidcraft stall, which they also wanted to continue to run within school as a contribution to the global concerns they had identified with. When community involvement of this nature is linked to learning then it arguably has more significance than a project which is an 'add on' to the curriculum, which may or may not have any meaning for pupils. That significance is partly related to the statement that this makes about learning and real life issues – the two are inevitably connected.

e) Values interventions can influence the ways pupils perceive the school's core values within the content and context of subjects within the school curriculum.

The outcomes of the Repertory Grid work provided evidence that these values interventions did influence the ways pupils used the school's core values in relation to the subject matter of the curriculum as well as the processes of learning in community. After the values interventions pupils generally thought the values were more relevant to the subject, and they described that relevance in a more discriminating way. To put it another way they used the values as constructs in a more sensitive and thoughtful manner – thus they had internalised the meaning and relevance of the values in a more sophisticated way.

During the second year of teaching and learning research the changes in the experimental group in science were even more significant. The control group showed no change in the ways in which they understood and thought about the values in relation to science, where as the experimental group showed a statistically significant change in the post-intervention grids.

A positive change in the ways in which pupils understand and apply the school's core values can be construed as development when that change is to understand the value and to apply it with more discrimination. In so far as the core values can be said to have spiritual, moral, social and cultural components to them, then values interventions can be said to promote spiritual, moral, social and cultural development of pupils. The emphasis on the *spirituality* or the *morality* of a core value might vary, and the *social* and *cultural* implications may be more or less evident, in the background or the foreground, but it is likely that all will be present in some degree. It is one of the central contentions of this work that these core values, located in community and a narrative tradition, provide an appropriate and meaningful vehicle for spiritual, moral, social and cultural development *because* they represent what the community perceives to be of 'ultimate truth, concern and value'.

5. Making Connections

a) Values interventions require teachers to set their lessons and their subjects into a more comprehensive understanding of how the world operates.

The teacher researchers found that in order to design and deliver a values intervention in their subject they had to move beyond their usual boundaries to more global concerns which might not normally appear in their teaching. Clark (Clark

1997) argues that a systems view of knowledge is important in enabling pupils to make sense out of their learning, and to make connections between otherwise discrete items of knowledge. He argues that there are some overarching principles and concepts that underpin all disciplines, and relate to global concerns. These include interdependence, sustainability, diversity, partnership, coevolution, fluctuating cycles and energy flow. These principles and concepts can be utilised to form a scaffolding for thinking about the subjects and are important components of developing 'systems thinking', or the science of the whole, rather than the science of the parts. Another way of putting this is to think about a 'top down' and a 'bottom up' approach to knowledge, the 'macro' or the 'micro' picture. Both are important, but the 'macro' picture locates the learning in a real life context which facilitates pupils making sense of their learning, and integrating it into their own life experience. Clark suggests that both approaches are important, and are not mutually exclusive. A systems approach to knowledge incorporates rather than replaces the analytical view of knowledge that has been dominant through the twentieth century, as part of the scientific and technological worldview.

The school's core values can be understood as overarching concepts, which are relevant to all of the disciplines, and which have an evaluative component to them.

Consistently, the values interventions designed by the teachers invited pupils to make connections between the discrete component of learning – such as blood transfusions, or road building or world war two – and a wider concerns such as justice, community, diversity, stewardship and social change. These wider concerns or values form part of the 'lifeworld' of individuals, communities and societies both present day, and historical, and as Habermas (Habermas 1973) argues, the hermeneutical rationality of the lifeworld is an intrinsic form in which knowledge is constituted, and through which human-beings come to make meaning out of life.

b) Values interventions add a spiritual dimension to lessons because they encourage a reflective searching for deeper meaning to events and issues.

Teachers found that the values interventions stimulated genuine discussion about 'ultimate concerns' and pupils often presented their own views on particular issues, whilst being challenged to think more deeply and in different ways about issues such as valuing others, or justice or truth. Spirituality – as the 'developing relationship of the individual, within community and tradition, to that which is - or is perceived to be - of ultimate concern, ultimate value and ultimate truth' can be fostered in many ways. Contrary to popular assumption, spirituality may be extremely 'earthy' and rooted into the 'messiness' and conflict of everyday life. Struggling with core values in relation to the self, to others and to God or another particular vision of life, is deeply spiritual within Wright's paradigm. Implicit in this paradigm is the notion of relationship – of the self with the self, of the self with others and of the self with that which is of ultimate concern.

The Platonic vision of 'surpassing' material things to reach the ultimate place of 'spirituality' has informed much western thinking and has left its legacy within the education system. Part of this legacy is the dualism of the 'sacred' and the 'secular' which pervades popular thinking, and is expressed in education in phrases such as the 'secular curriculum' as opposed to Religious Education and worship. The work done on this research project indicates that it is possible to operationalise an approach to spirituality in which it is integrated with everyday life and experience, and which can be understood as part of the generic nature of human life. Religious Education and worship play a particular and important role within this approach, but they do not define or monopolise the terrain.

c) Values interventions encourage critical thinking because they stimulate pupils to make judgements which require abstraction, reflection and

speculation. They also encourage an inter-disciplinary transfer of ideas and a holistic perspective on the curriculum.

The quality of discussion during values intervention lessons challenged pupils to search for meaning beyond the usual confines of the subject and to think about how they think. Taking a specific, practical event such as the building of the Great Western Railway, it was clear that there were differing levels of thinking and reflection involved and different types of learning resources needed. Firstly description and information about the events, then abstraction of the meaning and implications of the event, then reflection about those implications in the light of the community's commitment to the value of stewardship, and then speculation - the 'what if it had happened differently' sort of questions. This required imagination and creative thinking.

At the end of the second year of planned values interventions, the teacher researchers developed a typology of the thinking/learning strategies which were encouraged and were taking place during the interventions. They did this through their own observation and knowledge, through group assessment of pupils' work and through reference to the literature on thinking skills.

Learning Strategies, dispositions and qualities in values interventions

The following list of learning strategies, dispositions and qualities were identified as part of the 'terrain' of values interventions or of spiritual, moral, social and cultural development of pupils:

Critical thinking:

Learning how to question, when to question and what questions to ask – what are the problems?

Learning how to reason, when to reason and what reasoning methods to use.
Having a desire to reason, a desire for truth.
Being able to think independently.
Logical thinking.

Speculative thinking:

Thinking 'what if?' thinking about alternative options, futures thinking, thinking about hope, vision and the direction of social life.

Systems thinking:

Making connections between new information, existing experience, and wider cultural values.
Understanding worldviews - plurality and diversity.
Understanding the interconnectedness of the social and natural world.
Contextual thinking.
Perspectival intelligence.

Creative thinking:

Stimulus, exploration, planning, activity and review.
Making new connections, speculating, independent thinking, making personal value choices.

Thinking about thinking:

Self-aware reflection about how to form a view and make an independent decision.
Thinking about thinking about core values.

Emotional Intelligence:

Self-awareness, empathy, identity and toleration of ambiguity.
Intrapersonal and inter-personal intelligence.

Spiritual and moral intelligence:

Relationship of the pupil to the self, to others and to the Other or that which is of ultimate significance.
Vision and hope for a personal and social future.

6. Holistic Curriculum

a) Setting spiritual, moral, social and cultural development in the context of the whole curriculum framework avoids the separation of spiritual and moral development from its real life context. It also facilitates a more holistic relationship between pupils and teachers who attend to more than simply the pupil's cognitive needs

The teacher researchers found that dealing with the spiritual, moral, social and cultural issues which are implicit in their subjects in the context of learning about the subject was a meaningful and important way of both learning about the subject and developing pupils' spiritual and moral perceptions and skills. Pupils could generally see the relevance of the spiritual, moral, social and cultural issues to the subject, and teachers were able to relate to pupils more as whole people, with loves, hates, passions, commitments and idiosyncrasies. Although the research did not focus on the outcomes of values interventions in relation to pupils' expected learning outcomes in the particular subject, each teacher felt that pupils were more engaged with their learning in values interventions lessons. They felt that this would have an impact on how well they remembered the material and how they developed the ability to 'think' like a scientist, a musician or a historian. For example, a history intervention with year ten pupils entailed receiving Nazi propoganda about Jews without any prior discussion. The pupils found that the propoganda was having its intended effect on their attitudes and responses. When this was pointed out to them they were taken aback, and this then led to a 'engaged' discussion about truth, a careful scrutiny of the material and an analytical discussion about the validity of 'face value' impressions. The intervention was in fact a small adjustment to the normal approach, but it had a personal impact on the pupils. The ensuing discussion was described by some pupils as 'some of the best work they had done' and the teacher felt that this was because they were engaged emotionally with the ideas and were having to think for themselves. The historical skills of empathy, critical thinking and worldview analysis were brought into sharp focus in a meaningful way, and pupils began to form their own views and commitments to issues of racism and valuing others.

b) These core values can integrate well into the content of the subjects. Interventions can be readily designed (with appropriate resources). They frequently add a new dimension to the lessons because they draw upon wider cultural narratives and traditions and at the same time upon the pupils' own experience of life.

Before undertaking values interventions in lessons teachers needed to spend time familiarising themselves with the school's core values. The nature of these values, and their relationship to the whole school's vision, was explored and interpreted through dialogue amongst the teachers. There was not any attempt to dogmatically define and agree specific meanings for each of the values, rather through discussion and familiarisation each teacher came to their own understanding, which developed over time, and indeed through the interventions work itself.

The teachers did not find it difficult to design values interventions - the material is implicit in the subjects and in the processes of teaching and learning. However it often required the production of resources that was time consuming. Having completed the first year of the research the intervention lessons were written up in a common format and made available for other teachers to utilise as part of the 'roll out' phase of the programme. Use was made of commercially prepared materials, such as the CHARIS programme (Shortt 1996) with considerable success.

Teachers felt that values interventions added a new dimension to their teaching which they had not encountered before in their training or experience. They described the interventions as making their teaching more purposeful because it enabled them to think about the wider purposes and goals of education and to relate their subjects to real life issues and concerns.

c) There is a significant potential to deliver key aspects of citizenship through values interventions, in particular the components of moral and social development and community involvement. Values interventions are a means of naturally delivering some aspects of Personal and Social Education.

Every intervention delivered some of the key components of Citizenship as defined by the Crick Report and the Qualifications and Curriculum Authority documentation. Intervention lessons were also described by teachers as 'a very positive way to deliver personal and social education, with pupils they knew, and in relation to subjects with which they were familiar and which had real meaning for learning.

Each intervention was about moral and social development - although in this project that was not separated from spiritual development. Many of the interventions raised the possibility of developing community involvement, or service learning as a natural development.

It appeared that the spiritual component of the values interventions gave meaning to the moral, social and cultural components. The teachers understood spiritual development in various ways: searching for deeper meaning and purpose, passionate engagement against injustice, engagement with specific spiritual traditions. Broadly speaking spiritual development was understood to be taking place when pupils engaged as whole people with issues of ultimate concern within their tradition, and in relation to the material of their learning. For example, if a pupil experienced anger at the injustices experienced by Jewish people during the Holocaust, then the morality of being just in relationships in school and the wider community was a natural progression which had meaning to the pupil, and for which they had commitment and motivation.

d) Collaborative teamwork between practising teachers and academic researchers creates a potent research agenda and stimulates teacher professional development.

The research project developed over four years with a range of people, including students, governors, parents and teachers and it had serious commitment from the head teacher and senior management team of the school. Each year a team of up to six teachers (including at least one from the senior management team) were committed to the project at some level, and at least one remained engaged throughout.

At all the stages of the research design and implementation the meetings were school based and the research was incorporated into the school development plan. Teacher researchers, academic researchers and the Senior Management Team worked together to meet the school's needs. All parties attended all meetings. The Values Research team was given high profile by the Senior Management Team and through the School Development Plan and therefore the research was widely accepted and supported within the school.

The project was funded over the four years through small charitable grants from various sources, with a Teacher Training Agency project grant providing significant impetus for the project during its third year. The project was led by an education researcher who was able to put a significant amount of time into the project working with the teacher researchers, stimulating and developing the programme.

This collaborative approach has been viewed by the whole team as immensely productive, resulting in real input and changes for the school and its pupils as well as the development of key ideas as part of the research agenda. This has implications for teacher professional development and for research focused on improving teaching and learning outcomes through the collaboration of practitioners and researchers.

Characteristically teachers do not have much time to spare, especially for the sort of sustained reflection required by research. In addition teachers often view themselves as practitioners rather than academics – as though the two genres are mutually exclusive. Nearly all of the key ideas, strategies and analyses of this project have emerged through structured discussion with practising teachers – the researcher's task was to stimulate, structure and create space for those key ideas and insights to emerge, to develop them and to feed them back to the teachers.

7. The Ecology of Spiritual, Moral, Social and Cultural Development

The theme of 'connections' was pervasive in this project and many of the specific outcomes related to the idea of connecting things that would otherwise be seen separately. These connections could be, for example, the learners feelings with the learners cognitive capacities, or the learners own story with the material of learning, or the sacred with the secular or societies values with school's values and many more.

This was difficult to define but was considered by the 'researchers to be something approaching an understanding of the ecology of spiritual, moral, social and cultural development. There was a broad theme of enabling pupils to make connections between their own stories and experience, the wider traditions and cultural stories of the communities and the world in which they live in the context of their own development as learners, addressing the specific content of the curriculum.

The teachers found that developing the teaching and learning interventions through a set of core values which were drawn from the school community's vision encouraged them to think about the curriculum as a whole, rather than simply from the perspective of their own subject. It also enabled them to think about the learners as a whole, rather than from the perspective of their own subject or narrow definitions of intelligence.

The terrain into which this project led the project team seems to have a great deal in common with the terrain of lifelong learning, and learning to learn. As Claxton (1999)says:

> 'We have seen that the idea of intelligence as pre-eminently conscious, rational and articulate is undermined by evidence of the vital importance of the other, non-intellectual, compartments of the learning toolkit, and by demonstrations that hard thinking isn't very relevant to many of the smart things that real people do. The belief that a persons' learning power is fixed by some kind of general-purpose intelligence has had to give way to the idea of a flexible and learnable repertoire of mental strategies. We have seen that the idea that intelligence is purely cognitive – that it can be divorced from people's qualities, values, beliefs, dispositions and personalities – is also invalid. Ability is a function of the whole person. And now we can see that intelligence isn't even a personal possession, but rather a floating conglomerate of resources that are external as well as internal' (226)

Chapter Nine
The UK National Policy Context

1. Introduction

The preamble to the 1988 Education Reform Act states that the purpose of education is 'to promote the spiritual, moral, cultural, mental and physical development of pupils at school and of society......and to prepare pupils for he opportunities, responsibilities and experiences of adult life'. These broad aims were not new, echoing the 1944 Education Act, and were intended provide a rationale which underpinned the whole curriculum. Chadwick (Chadwick 1997) refers to these aspirations in the 1988 Act as seemingly impressive 'until the reality became [clear], that schools struggling just to comply with the law on National Curriculum attainment targets had little scope to reflect on these broader cross curricular themes and dimensions'. In reality these twin aims had little impact on schooling, where the dominant policy agenda of improving measurable standards within a 'quasi-market' of schools proved to be all consuming.

However the legislation which did prove to bring the issue of spiritual, moral, social and cultural development of pupils onto the actual policy agenda of schools, was the 1992 Education Act which set out the criteria for inspection of schools by the newly formed Office for Standards in Education (OFSTED). The government intended that schools would be inspected on their ability to deliver educational standards; their ability to function with efficiency and their effectiveness as educational institutions.

The inclusion of a requirement for OFSTED to report upon the spiritual, moral, social and cultural development of pupils were amendments introduced by Lord Northbourne in the House of Lords. They were introduced as a strategy to balance the dominant focus in education policy on raising standards, and improving learning outcomes for pupils, measured quantitatively, without giving due attention to the wider processes and social contexts in which learning takes place including the spiritual and moral formation of pupils. It was also a challenge to a powerful educational myth of the twentieth century that schools could be 'value neutral' places, and that questions of value and belief should be left at the door of the school room and only addressed at home.

The amendments were vigorously rejected by the government, whose apprehension was that pupils might be encouraged to question 'too critically' (ibid) as a result. Interestingly, however, the House of Lords was strongly in favour and after 'enormous battles' the government was overturned and the legislation went through onto the statute books (Walford 1995). The spirit of the amendments was welcomed by all sides of the upper house – regardless of political party or religious persuasions.

At the same time the government was preparing its 1992 White Paper. It is quite likely that the House of Lords debate stimulated the Secretary of State, John Patten to include explicit reference to the importance of spiritual and moral development in schools. It also included an unprecedented assertion of the belief that values of all sorts shape practice in schooling. Chapter Eight, widely reputed to have been written by the Secretary of State for Education himself, declares 'Education cannot and must not be value-free' and it goes on to introduce the arrangements for schools to be inspected specifically on the spiritual and moral development of their pupils (Department 1992).

The controversy and heated debate surrounding these issues, which can be traced right through to Curriculum 2000 and the introduction of Citizenship education indicates the deep confusion and uncertainty which exists regarding spiritual and moral development, and the key question of whose values, and whose vision should shape schools in the modern context.

A parallel policy initiative, embraced by the neo-conservative wing of the Tory party was to do with collective worship and Religious Education. This was highly controversial. A central aspect of that debate surrounded the relationship between spirituality and religion, and the specific role of the Christian religion in schools in a society where the Christian Church is privileged, but the majority of the population do not regularly attend a Christian church. The outcome was that the statutory daily act of worship, and Religious Education should 'gives proper regard to the nation's Christian heritage and traditions' (ibid p37). This debate was important in its own right but generated as much heat as light, and in many ways served only to confuse the issues about spiritual, moral, social and cultural development of pupils. This was because it was dealing with only one aspect of the curriculum, ie Religious Education and Worship, which could not avoid questions of confessionalism and the plural – multi-faith and secularised – nature of British society. It was easy for this debate to be dominated by the religious right and an authoritarian Christianity that could be supported by the statutory framework – which appeared to be the antithesis of the liberal ideal of individual freedom and tolerance.

The Northbourne amendments however, challenged the 'spiritual and moral neutrality' of the whole of the curriculum of schools, and did not promote or privilege any particular worldview or religious position. They did not dictate any particular content, but rather the idea that the spiritual, moral, social and cultural development of pupils was an essential component of ethical educational provision in a modern and diverse society which must be given due attention by schools. They could be addressed with equal integrity by faith-based and secular schools.

As a result of the amendments the OFSTED Inspection Framework was amended in 1993 to combine all four areas of personal development – spiritual, moral, social and cultural. The 1995 revision asked inspectors to judge the extent to which a school was providing its pupils 'with knowledge and insight into values and beliefs and enable[d] them to reflect on their experiences in a way which develop[ed] their spiritual awareness and self-knowledge' (section 5.3).

A discussion document on Spiritual and Moral Development was produced by the National Curriculum Council in 1993 (NCC 1993). This aimed to demonstrate to schools that spiritual and moral development was not only the domain of Religious Education and Collective Worship but to all aspects of school life and all aspects of the curriculum. The discussion paper emphasised

> *'The potential for spiritual development is open to everyone and is not confined to the development of religious beliefs or conversion to a particular faith.....It has to do with relationships with other people.....the search for meaning and purpose in life and for values by which to live'.*

The OFSTED Framework 2000 (OFSTED 2000) includes requirements for inspectors to evaluate and report upon pupils' attitudes, values and personal development. In relation to the curriculum inspectors are required evaluate and report upon how well schools cultivate pupils' personal – including spiritual, moral, social and cultural -development. In addition they are required to consider the extent to which the curriculum amongst other things:

> *'provides pupils with knowledge and insights into values and beliefs, and enables them to reflect on their experiences in a way which develops their spiritual awareness and self knowledge'* and

> *'Promotes principles which distinguish right from wrong'* and

> *'Encourages pupils to take responsibility, show initiative and develop an understanding of living in a community'*
> p39

2. The National Forum for Values in Education and the Community

The controversy and debate about the spiritual and moral education of young people was both stimulated and fuelled by some dramatic and tragic events which were seen as somehow symptomatic of a more general malaise within society about spiritual and moral values. The murder of Jamie Bulger, and of headteacher Philip Lawrence stood out in public consciousness as shocking events that were indicative somehow of the spiritual and moral uncertainty of the age and of the presence of 'evil' within society despite the advances of knowledge and technology and the experiences of the 20th century.

In 1996 a National Symposium initiated by the School Curriculum and Assessment Authority, and attended by Sir Ron Dearing and Dr Nick Tate – the Chairman and Chief Executive – began a process of national consultation on 'the spiritual and moral dimensions of the curriculum'.   The conference agreed that a Forum should be set up with a two-fold remit:

- To discover whether there are any values upon which there is agreement across society
- To decide how best society in general, and SCAA in particular might support schools in the task of promoting pupils' spiritual, moral, social and cultural development (Talbot 1997)

The Forum had 150 members drawn from across society and they emerged with a number of values to which, they believed, everyone would subscribe regardless of race, ethnic group, religion age or class (see appendix). This was conclusively established by a MORI omnibus poll of 1500 adults that drew a 95% agreement with those values.

The Forum did not claim that there was agreement about the *source* of those values or the *belief systems* or *worldviews* from which they were derived. Talbot and Tate argued too, that these values *are* obvious, and that they *do* smack of 'motherhood and apple pie' - but that over the last decade society has focused so hard, and for good reasons, on difference, that we have become blind to our common humanity.

This consultation was a key landmark in the policy story because it established that there are in fact certain ethical values that have the authority of consensus. It raised the level of debate through a wide consultation process and began to clear some of the muddy waters and begin to open up the very real question about whose vision and whose values should schools be promoting in a postmodern, plural society.

A further development of this forum was that the newly established Qualifications and Curriculum Authority (replacing SCAA) appointed Marianne Talbot to develop guidance for schools on implementing a whole school framework for spiritual, moral, social and cultural development of pupils. This guidance was developed in a pilot phase beginning in January 1998. Two hundred schools received the guidance 'cold'; fifty schools received the guidance with support from LEAs and the QCA. This case study described in this book was an independent 'in-depth' project which began with close reference to the QCA guidance, and which aimed to contribute to the process both in terms of its findings and the eventual case study report. The QCA pilot phase was expected to last for two years and the outcomes were expected to inform the final production of guidance for schools as part of Curriculum 2000.

3. Preparation for Adult Life Initiatives and Citizenship Education

The advent of a labour government in 1997 brought some new currents to the policy process in relation to spiritual, moral, social and cultural development of pupils and values education. Principally this was a strong interest in, and commitment to, the notion of citizenship education held by the new Secretary of State for Education, and his mentor on citizenship, Professor Bernard Crick. The Advisory Group on Citizenship was established following the White Paper, Excellence in Schools, which worked from the following terms of reference:

> *'To provide advice on effective education for citizenship in schools – to include the nature and practises of participation in democracy; the duties, responsibilities and rights of individuals as citizens; and the value to individuals and society of community activity'.*

This Advisory Group, chaired by Bernard Crick, produced its report 'Education for Citizenship and teaching of democracy in schools in 1998. This report formed the basis for the subsequent citizenship orders in 1999.

The period leading up to Curriculum 2000 was characterised by fragmentation and strongly motivated interest groups competing for access to policy formation. There were those interested in Personal, Social and Health Education, Creativity, Citizenship, spiritual, moral, social and cultural development and others. All of these differing interest groups were brought together under the umbrella of a 'Preparation for Adult Life Group' (PAL) whose remit was to inform the review of the National Curriculum in relation to those aspects of the curriculum that directly contribute to the 'preparation for adult life'. Given the genuinely critical nature of the general debate, the strength of feeling and commitment from various groups to their differing angles on the topic, and the natural desire on the part of a new government to make a distinctive mark, this period was fraught with uncertainty and speculation.

4. Curriculum 2000 - values and aims.

The outcomes of the deliberations of the PAL group became clear with the publication of the revised National Curriculum. As Tate (Tate 2000) argues one weakness of the old National Curriculum was that it told teachers what they had to teach, but failed to tell them why. Thus Curriculum 2000 includes an introductory rationale which is explicit about the role of values and purposes. It is as follows:

'RATIONALE FOR THE SCHOOL CURRICULUM AND FUNCTIONS OF THE NATIONAL CURRICULUM

Values and purposes underpinning the school curriculum

Education influences and reflects the values of society, and the kind of society we want ourselves to be. It is important, therefore, to recognise a broad set of common values and purposes which underpin the school curriculum and the work of schools.

Foremost is a belief in education, at home and at school, as a route to spiritual, moral, social, cultural, physical and mental development, and thus the well being, of the individual. Education is also a route to equality of opportunity for all, a healthy and just democracy, a productive economy, and sustainable development. Education should reflect the enduring values that contribute to these ends. These include valuing ourselves, our families and other relationships, the wider groups to which we belong, the diversity in our society and the environment in which we live.* Education should also

---

* In planning their curriculum schools may wish to take into account the statement of values
(May 1997) finalised after widespread consultation by the National Forum for Values in
Education and the Community.

reaffirm our commitment to the virtues of truth, justice, honesty, trust and a sense of duty.

At the same time education must enable us to respond positively to the opportunities and challenges of the rapidly changing world in which we live and work. In particular, we need to be prepared to engage as individuals, parents, workers and citizens with new work and leisure patterns resulting from economic, social and cultural change, the continued globalisation of the economy and society and with the rapid expansion of communication technologies.

Aims for the school curriculum

The school curriculum covers the totality of children's experiences in, or connected with, schools. If schools are to respond to the values and purposes effectively, schools, working in collaboration with families and the local community, including church and voluntary groups, local agencies and business, should seek to achieve two broad aims through the curriculum. These aims provide an essential context within which schools develop their own curriculum.

(i)   The school curriculum should aim to provide opportunities for all pupils to learn and to achieve.

The curriculum should develop pupils' enjoyment of, and commitment to, learning as a means of encouraging and stimulating the best possible progress and the highest attainment for all pupils. It should build on pupils' strengths, interests and experiences and develop their confidence in their capacity to learn and work independently and collaboratively. It should equip pupils with the essential learning skills of literacy, numeracy, and information and communication technology, and promote an enquiring mind and capacity to think rationally.

The school curriculum should contribute to the development of pupils' sense of identity through knowledge and understanding of the spiritual, moral, social and cultural heritages of Britain's diverse society and of the local, national, European, Commonwealth and global dimensions of their lives. It should encourage pupils to appreciate human aspirations and achievements in aesthetic, scientific, technological and social fields, and prompt a personal response to a range of experiences and ideas.

By providing rich and varied contexts for pupils to acquire, develop and apply a broad range of knowledge, understanding and skills, the curriculum should enable pupils to think creatively and critically, to solve problems and to make a difference for the better. It should give them the opportunity to become creative, innovative and enterprising, and capable of leadership to equip them for their future lives as workers and citizens. It should also develop their physical skills and encourage them to recognise the importance of pursuing a healthy lifestyle and keeping themselves and others safe.

(ii)   The school curriculum should aim to promote pupils' spiritual, moral, social and cultural development and prepare all pupils for the opportunities, responsibilities and experiences of life.

The school curriculum should promote pupils' spiritual, moral, social and cultural development and, in particular, develop principles for distinguishing between right and wrong. It should develop their knowledge, understanding and appreciation of their own and different beliefs and cultures, and how these influence individuals and societies. The school curriculum should pass on enduring values, develop pupils' integrity and autonomy and help them to be responsible and ·caring citizens capable of contributing to the development of a just society. It should promote equal opportunities and enable pupils to challenge discrimination and stereotyping. It should develop their awareness, understanding, and respect for the environments in which they live, and secure their commitment to sustainable development at a personal, local, national and global level. It should also equip pupils as consumers to make informed judgements and independent decisions and to understand their responsibilities and rights.

It should promote pupils' self-esteem and emotional well-being and help them to form and maintain worthwhile and satisfying relationships, based on respect for themselves and for others, at home, at school, at work and in the community. It should develop their ability to relate to others and work for the common good.   It should enable pupils to respond positively to opportunities, challenges and responsibilities, to manage risk and to cope with change and adversity.

It should prepare pupils for the next steps in their learning, training and employment and equip them to make informed choices at school and throughout their lives, enabling them to appreciate the relevance of their achievements to life and society outside school, including leisure, community engagement and employment.

These two aims reinforce each other.   The personal development of pupils, spiritually, morally, socially and culturally, plays a significant part in their ability to learn and to achieve.   Development in both areas is essential to raising standards of attainment for all pupils.'
(DFEE 2000)

This framework gives explicit affirmation of the key role of values and spiritual, moral, social and cultural development in schools and in learning. It is significant because it requires schools to look at the curriculum as a whole and to think about questions of ultimate concern or values. One of the dangers of the various policy initiatives which came under the PAL umbrella was that they would be seen by schools as fragmented from each other, and also as discrete entities to be 'added on' to an already overcrowded curriculum. However the current framework mitigates against this danger and creates a platform for schools to be holistic and professional in their approach and to operationalise their own community's distinctive vision and values.

5. Links between citizenship and spiritual, moral, social and cultural development of pupils.

Tate (Tate 2000) refers to citizenship as being essentially about values. It asserts the value of being informed, critical and responsible; that we should respect other peoples' identities and that it is a good thing to be reflective. It is about promoting and transmitting those values which are the shared values of our society.

Both OFSTED and initially the QCA have tended to deal with spiritual, moral, social and cultural development as four separate entities, which should be treated separately. However one of the key points in this case study research was in the realisation that each of the school's core values, identified by the community, had spiritual, moral, social and cultural aspects to them. Thus whenever a core value was fore-grounded in teaching and learning some or all of spiritual, moral, social and cultural development may have been taking place. In addition as the research team evaluated the values interventions, it was clear that, without exception, they made a contribution to citizenship education – in terms of knowledge, understanding, skills, values and attitudes.

Thus the notion of values is the common factor between citizenship and spiritual, moral, social and cultural development of pupils. However these values are not 'free floating' values, unrelated to the life and experience and traditions of pupils in schools. Values are actually embedded in discourses, traditions, narratives or worldviews which are 'lived and experienced' by real human beings who constitute the institutions, including the schools, which form the structure of society. Thus the notion of values is also a common factor between the school, its own vision and leadership and the wider community of institutions and associations which form the fabric of society.

6. The Citizenship Framework

The Crick Report remained the basis for the Citizenship framework published as a statutory part of the National Curriculum for Key Stages three and four and part of the recommended framework for Key Stages one and two.

It identifies three strands that constitute effective education for citizenship, which should be evident in all Key Stages. These are

- social and moral responsibility;
- community involvement and
- political literacy.

The essential elements of citizenship are implicit in the aims and purposes of citizenship education and also implicit in the three strands. These elements are

- Concepts
- Values and dispositions
- Skills and aptitudes
- Knowledge and understanding

These elements are inter-related and should be approached in a developmental and sequential way through the four key stages. There are three modes through which citizenship can be delivered through the curriculum. These are through discrete curriculum time, allocated specifically to 'citizenship'; through particular activities that are additional to the curriculum; and through provision within the wider subjects of the curriculum.

One of the key ideas behind citizenship education, is that it 'is about a proper balance between knowledge, understanding, skills, values and attitudes and its success will depend on the interaction of all of these elements' (Tate 2000).

Discrete curriculum provision is likely to be critical for the delivery of some of the concepts, knowledge and understanding elements of citizenship, particularly within the political literacy strand. In practice, however, this is likely to be a part of a re-formulate PSHE programme at secondary level because of the constraints of time-tabling. However a very substantial part of citizenship education can be addressed through all of the subjects of the curriculum and through additional community involvement projects or 'service learning'.

7. Case Study Findings

In the case study school, each values intervention addressed the 'moral and social' strand of the citizenship framework – although significantly this was not at the expense of the spiritual given the understanding of the nature of spirituality described earlier. There is thus considerable overlap between the domains we have come to call 'spiritual, moral, social and cultural development', 'citizenship education', 'values education' and Personal, Social and Health Education and Religious Education. The coherence of these domains within any particular school depends upon the location of them all within a whole school framework, where the overarching vision and values of the school provide the starting point and a frame of reference.

The following chart simply lists some differing groups of values and concepts from the case study school, the Institute for Global Ethics, Rationale for the National Curriculum and the Citizenship Framework. The point is simply to highlight the areas of overlap between citizenship, spiritual, moral, social and cultural development of pupils and values education. They are perhaps all really different facets of the same thing – that 'same thing' being the 'softer' side of schooling or the moral vision and purpose which needs to underpin and permeate the whole enterprise if it is to be meaningful and capable of adaptation to the demands of the 21st century.

	Institute for Global Ethics Core Values		Citizenship Values & Dispositions	Citizenship Concepts	(Clark 1997)'s overarching concepts
	Respect for life		Human dignity and equality Human rights	Democracy and autocracy Rights and responsibilities	Interdependence
	Responsibility		Proclivity to act responsibly Concern for the environment	Co-operation and conflict	Sustainability
	Fairness Freedom Unity Tolerance		Concern for common good Concern to resolve conflict Empathy Tolerance Respect for the rule of law Determination to act justly Commitment to active citizenship Equal opportunities Voluntary service	Fairness, justice the rule of law, rules, law and human rights Freedom and order	Diversity Partnership
	Truthfulness		Critical openness Individual initiative and effort	Individual and community	Fluctuating cycles
				Power and authority	Co-evolution
	Love		Faith in a liberal democracy		Energy flow

These concepts and values indicate the terrain of a wider and deeper discourse which is possible and desirable in education policy – whether that is at a school level or at the level of national policy formation. They indicate the centrality of the learning process, which is hopefully the same as the schooling process, to the health and well-being of society. In someways this terrain also marks out the 'lifeworld' of schooling – that which human beings apprehend through a form of rationality which is different to the means-end, strategic rationality of measurable learning outcomes, increased economic productivity, and raised standards which distinguish so much of contemporary policy discourse. It also indicates a critical area of professionalism - that of ethical educational leadership.

Rabbi Sacks draws upon the Judaic vision of citizenship education as a model from which we can learn. He argues that what is compelling about this vision is that it places education at the very heart of the society-building enterprise. Education, he argues, is a significant counter-force to the other two great and dominant factors in society. Firstly government, politics and the distribution of power and secondly markets, economics and the distribution of wealth. (Sacks 2000). He argues that the idea central to the Jewish vision is that learning is a lifelong process, which is built around the community – the synagogue, the home and the school.

He underlines the importance of the question with which this book began. What gods or stories are being served by contemporary education? A critical and coherent approach to values in schools, incorporating citizenship and spiritual, moral, social and cultural development of pupils, and engaging with the community, will enable school leaders to regain some professionalism in terms of aims and purposes and to make a significant contribution to the critical and lifelong process of learning which is essential for a healthy society.

Chapter Ten
Critical Issues

1. Introduction

There are a number of critical issues that are central to the concerns of this book. The case study researchers approached the project from an empirical perspective, basing their developing ideas on close observation and evaluation of what actually takes place in the school and in the classroom. Inevitably and appropriately teachers are concerned with practice, with what works, and with common sense application. Furthermore no researchers arrive at a research question free of presuppositions, blind spots and pre-conceived ideas – this is as much the case with theoretical work as with empirical work. Reflection on the wider theoretical issues took place within the research as a response to findings in practice – in an effort to make sense of what was understood to be taking place. These factors have to be taken into account in any evaluation of this project, and in any claims that can be made on the basis of this work.

This final chapter begins to identify some of the critical issues that are embedded in this aspect of education, and it does so within the holistic framework established over the period of the work. In a substantial review of recent research in this field (Halstead 2000) Halstead and Taylor say

> *'Research on the development of pupils' values attitudes and personal qualities is replete with complex, ongoing debates and issues, often with a theoretical basis and with fundamental implications for educational policy, school structures and strategies, and teaching practices.'*
> *P 15*

They list some of the unresolved contemporary questions, which touch upon the following areas - relativism and absolutism; consensus and pluralism; whose values? what values?; gender and moral orientation; cognition, emotion and action; teachers' values; aims and outcomes and parents and schools.

This chapter will be structured by addressing three overarching themes. Firstly the key question of whose vision and values, which will take us into a discussion about pluralism, consensus, communitarianism, and the 'lifeworld' of contemporary culture. Secondly the question of spirituality and its relationship to citizenship and to religion. Finally the question of learning in the 21st century and the role of cognition, emotion, worldviews and spiritual and moral development.

2. Whose vision and whose values?

In an age of uncertainty, and both secularised and multi-faith societies, this question is of critical importance. It is probably true that when the UK 1944 Education Act was established there was a widespread consensus that spiritual and moral development, collective worship and Religious Education would be based upon a Judeo Christian framework. The Act itself constituted a settlement with the Churches creating the Voluntary Aided and Controlled sector of schools within a national framework. Since then processes of secularisation, immigration and globalisation have altered the fabric of communities and of society, making it impossible to justify the state 'imposing' any one particular religion, worldview or set of religious values, through education.

At the same time the state has increased substantively its control over schooling. The national curriculum, the inspection framework and funding arrangements all indicate a far greater control of education and schooling by government than has ever existed before. Schools are required to be self-managing, but the focus of the policy of self-management of schools is on the strategic control of objectified processes in the service of effectiveness and efficiency. It is not upon the communal self-management of the particular school's vision and values and a distinctive understanding of its own educational purposes and goals. (Deakin Crick 1996) This form of self management I refer to as 'hermeneutical' self management, which is drawn from a Habermasian notion of 'hermeneutical rationality' as one anthtropologically deep seated human interest, alongside 'strategic rationality' and 'emancipatory rationality.

This notable absence in the discourse of self management, coupled with the confusion about values and purposes characteristic of contemporary education, means that external values and discourses continue to profoundly shape practice in schools. Schools are never value free; the question is not whether they are transmitting values, worldviews, ultimate concerns and spirituality, but what values, worldviews, ultimate concerns and spirituality are they transmitting?

In a study of the policy of self management of schools, (ibid), which included a critical discourse analysis of leading policy makers' language relating to self management and diversity, the dominant worldview, or discourse, which was shaping practice in the case study schools was that of liberalism, informed by the discourse of the 'free market' and the needs of the nation state to secure its economic future. Within this discourse the person is an autonomous agent, the individual and the state are flip sides of the same coin, and values are separate from facts.

Thus the question about whose vision and whose values should determine the practice of schools takes on a different shape because it s not a question about what additional, but non-essential moral values can be 'added on to the central task of schooling'. Rather it becomes a matter of professional educational ethics that all schools are explicit and responsible about the values they promote and nurture. The question then becomes who should participate in the process of identifying those values? Which individuals, groups or communities are authoritative in this respect?

3. Communitarianism and Liberalism

It is at this point that the current debate between the liberals and communitarians becomes highly relevant. In recent years, according to Delaney (Delaney 1994), the debate between the liberals and the communitarians has been the central debate in political philosophy. He compares a general liberal perspective, promoted by Rawls, Nozick and Dworkin with a general communitarian perspective shared by MacIntyre, Taylor and Sandel. Communitarianism is seen as a substantive and crucial challenge to the individualist, rights-based contractarian liberalism, which has been most significantly expounded by Rawls (Rawls 1971). It has developed from a view that gives fuller expression to the claims of citizenship and community than the liberal vision allows and embodies a different conception of the person. The liberal Kantian view of the self is as a choosing self, independent of the desires and ends it may have at any moment. 'The self is prior to the ends which are affirmed by it; even a dominant end must be chosen from among numerous possibilities' (ibid p560). The right is prior to the good. However the communitarian position is that we cannot conceive of ourselves as independent in such a way - wholly detached from our aims and attachments. There are social attachments that determine the self and thus individuals are constituted by the community of which they are a part. Sandel (Sandel 1984) postulates the image of a person with 'constitutive ends', those ends which constitute who the person is, and MacIntyre (MacIntyre 1992) similarly argues that one understands one's life only by looking at ones actions within a 'narrative' which converges with the 'narratives' of other people, who come to be part of one's own narrative. Thus an understanding of oneself can only be attained in the context of community.

Moody (Moody 1994) construes the hallmark of communitarianism to be its metaphysics of the state, the individual and their relationship. Communitarianism rejects liberal atomism and the characteristic Hobbesian moral individualism that posits the antagonism between individuals as the basis of society. Rather he sees the fundamental relationship between the individual and society as 'mutual aid' and insists that at all levels of political analysis the self must be the actual self, embedded in a culture and with corrigible desires and beliefs. Thus a Kantian notion of respect for persons is inadequate. A respect for persons can be generated from a communitarian basis but not in the atomistic style favoured by liberalism. Thus communitarians are attempting to reconstruct important political ideals such as respect for persons, justice and liberty that is based on a relational self and a non-foundationalist epistemology. Moody considers three types of social bonds: self-interest, obligation and communal and mutual bonds, the latter of which have been the subject of much recent feminist discussion. He goes on to say

> *'...communitarianism holds that liberal theory relies much too heavily on bonds of the first two types and has little theoretical space for bonds of mutuality. Whereas liberal theory has tended to relegate communal bonds to the private realm of friendship and the family and to see the public realm as characterised by self-interest and obligation, communitarians believe that public relationships must be seen as, to some extent, mutual and not exclusively instrumental or impartially obligatory. These mutualistic public relations must be seen as a constitutive element of who we are, the public analog to such private relationships as friendship and love' (Moody ibid p93).*

Communitarianism includes methodological and normative arguments and moral and political claims. What most of its scholars, both radical and conservative, share is the advocacy of involvement in public life, the importance of participation in small communities, firms and clubs. They see these 'mediating structures' (mediating between the individual and the state) as safeguards against the potential totalitarianism of the state which might result from the 'politics of the common good' rather than the politics of individual rights.

There are clearly connections here between the claims of communitarians and Habermas's communicative ethics, in which Habermas sets the debate in terms of the task of the problem of mediation between Moralitat and Sittliechkeit, that is in White's words

> *'between the part of morality which deals with universalistic criteria of justice and the abstract judging of institutional orders on the one hand, and the part which encompasses concrete relationships and value configurations peculiar to given forms of life, on the other'* (White 1988) *p85*

Within a communitarian framework, individuals only are what they are by their inherence in a community, which is the ground of their identity. In important ways, human identity is expressed in relation to others within community, and communities share ideas, beliefs, values, traditions as well as vision and aspiration. Taylor argues that

> *'One of the great needs of the modern democratic polity is to recover a sense of significant differentiation, so that its partial communities, be they geographical, or cultural, or occupational, can become again important centres of concern and activity which connects them to the whole' (Taylor 1984) p197.*

4. Schools as Partial Communities

Schools are important centres of community. A community has at least three major elements. Firstly a territorial element - it refers to a group of people who live and work within a particular geographical area, whether that is a local residential area, or a wider part of a city or country. With the advent of the Internet, it is possible to have geographically dispersed, or virtual communities. A second element comprises the social structures which form communities - principally families, schools, businesses, services, churches, mosques and voluntary associations. The third, and perhaps most significant element in this analysis is the relational element. This refers to those factors that cause the other elements to cohere as a community. It will encompass shared interests, tasks and purposes, values and norms for human conduct, which form the culture or sub-cultures of communities.

Schools as communities have geographical territories. They have internal and external social structures that regulate them and enable them to function. They have shared aims and purposes, interests and values and they are constituted by relationships of all sorts. Those interest groups that participate in schooling include children, their parents and families, local and national government, churches, businesses, other social agencies and voluntary associations.

It is quite appropriate from a communitarian perspective to argue that the school community itself has the responsibility to identify its vision and the core values which it will be guided by in its practice, and the belief system, worldview/s and traditions which underpin it. That vision and those values should inform and shape the school's approach to spiritual, moral, social and cultural development of pupils and citizenship. Any consultation or investigation into vision and values should include all stakeholders and each school, like each family or business, is likely to be distinctive in some way from other schools.

Schools also have different foundations, and in the case of Church schools and schools with a distinctive religious or philosophical foundation, there are structural and legal requirements to take into account the 'voice' of the particular religious or philosophical tradition. In the UK there is increasing pressure for the 7000 publicly funded Church schools to show how and in what ways they are distinctive.

The entire enterprise is significantly regulated by the government both in the public and the private sector by the national framework for schools and also by equal opportunities legislation, human rights, health and safety regulations etc. All of these factors create a strong, structural framework which militates against extreme diversity or extremism of any sort, and which actually encourages uniformity. For example it would be illegal for a school to formally identify white supremacy as a core value, even if the entire community actually lived that value. Similarly prohibitions exist against discrimination on the grounds of gender, disability and faith.

Each stakeholder, whether pupil, teacher, governor or policy maker is a person-in – relation who is significantly constituted by the social and cultural communities of which she or he is a part. Whatever an individual's particular worldview or belief system that person will be shaped by prevailing cultural attitudes, beliefs and values in an organic and dynamic process. Whatever its distinctive vision and values, schools will inevitably be connected to the 'whole', i.e. concerns and values which relate to the nation, and the globe because its constituent groups are peopled by people who are connected to the nation and the globe. Indeed, schools as communities are perhaps very important locations for the expression of the 'mutualistic public bonds' which are important counter balances to the instrumental and obligatory nature of public relationships.

In the context of 'self management' the actual responsibility for the nature and conduct of schools rests with the governing body or school board, within a national framework. The school board is constituted to be representative of those groups which have a legitimate interest in schooling, which can include Churches. This is consistent with a theology of work in which authority is consistent with responsibility and calling – put simply, God calls school people to run schools, not politicians, Church leaders, business people or others.

5. Spirituality, Religion & the spiritual, moral, social and cultural development of pupils.

In order to be hermeneutically self-managing, schools need a robust understanding of questions of values, spirituality, morality and the 'softer side' of schooling. Fullan's (Fullan

1993) exploration of educational reforms over the last thirty years led him to the conclusion that we have been 'fighting an ultimately fruitless uphill battle'. He argues that rather than introducing more innovations and reforms into the system we actually need to develop a new mindset about educational change. That mindset is one in which managing moral purpose and change agency is at the heart of productive educational change. These two factors have an explicit and organic relationship. At the heart of teaching is moral purpose – a vision about 'the good life', a focus on ultimate questions of meaning and purpose. In his later work Fullan (Fullan 1999) uses the language of spirituality interchangeably with the language of 'moral purpose', a move which is consistent with the working definition of spirituality used shortly in this paper.

The distinction between spirituality and religion is important in this debate. In 'Virtual Faith' Beaudoin (Beaudoin 1998) tends to use the word 'religiousness' when referring to the spirituality of generation X because of the common association of the word religion with a particular institution. He argues that a key component of religiousness, or spirituality, is a profound experience of a limitation.

This understanding of religiousness is consistent with Tillich (Tillich 1959) who calls this sense of religiousness 'the aspect of depth in the totality of the human spirit' and this points to what is 'ultimate, infinite, unconditional' (p7). Spirituality, or religiousness, is not therefore confined to a particular religion, and to the extent that a sense of the ultimate can be held without the concept of God, it is a property of all human beings.

This notion of spirituality is important, although problematic, in a condition of post –modernity. These ideas are not new in education in the UK. In fact the HMI discussion paper Curriculum 11-16 offers a definition of the spiritual area of experience which is anthropological in its focus.

'The spiritual area is concerned with the awareness a person has of those elements in existence and experience which may be defined in terms of inner feelings and beliefs; they affect the way people see themselves and throw light for them on the purpose and meaning of life itself. Often these feelings and beliefs lead people to claim to know God and glimpse the transcendent; sometimes they represent that striving and longing for perfection which characterises human beings, but always they are concerned with matters at the heart and root of existence.'

These attempts to articulate a common universal definition into which all pupils may be inducted reflects an attempt to identify the universal anthropological and epistemological structures of spirituality. The spiritual dimension is an integral part of human nature and spirituality itself is experiential and related to transcendence, universality, value and mystery. It gives primacy to the process of spiritual sensibility – questions of content, knowledge and truth are secondary.

It represents a challenge to the legacy of unbridled rationalism of modernity, and echoes both progressive/romantic critiques of education and post-modern critiques. The former asserts the primacy of feeling over reason, and the latter deconstructs all forms of rational thought (Wright 1998).

It is an understanding of spirituality that represents a contemporary consensus. It is re-affirmed in the National Curriculum Council discussion paper (NCC 1993) and in subsequent policy documents. Although primarily developed within the discipline of Religious Education in schools, it is becoming universalised as spiritual development is increasingly understood to be a cross-curricular theme that can and should permeate all subjects of the curriculum. It is attractive politically because it an apparent liberal affirmation of religious diversity, and a negation of the dominant mainstream roots of one religion – the Christian tradition – in British society.

In the UK, each school is inspected upon its capacity to 'deliver' spiritual, moral, social and cultural development of pupils within all of the subjects of the taught curriculum, as well as the general ethos of the school. According to the new rationale for the National Curriculum 2000 the school's own vision and values should inform that spiritual and moral development. In addition, from 2002, all schools will have to teach citizenship, which includes community involvement, moral and social development and political literacy.

This discourse of spirituality is one in which there are significant problems. As Wright (Wright 1998) argues, the contemporary consensus on spiritual pedagogy is actually framed within the modernistic thought forms that it is seeking to counter. It is dependent on, and thus reflects the flaws of, the very culture it seeks to undermine. It is actually a particular spiritual tradition arising from western culture's response to the fragmentation of the narratives of modernity.

> *'Far from uncovering a universal dimension of human spiritual potential, the contemporary educational discourse must be read as rooted in provincial attempt within the modern western intellectual tradition to escape the excesses of modernity. It does this by identifying and challenging the authoritarian rationalism of the modern idealistic and empirical traditions, and by supplementing them with a romantic critique. It further rejects an authoritarian influence within romanticism itself by asserting the postmodern belief that romantic sensibility must be reduced series of relativistic cultural games, ones always localised and dependent upon the individual freedom to construct perceptions of reality at will, unconstrained by any universal claims implied by the romantic tradition'*
> *(ibid p68)*

Wright goes on to argue that this discourse of spirituality is not capable of being a generic discourse because, for example, when contrasted with orthodox Christian spirituality it is found to be incompatible with the notion of personhood, and the truth claims in which orthodox Christianity is located. The dominant discourse of spirituality in education actually nurtures children in a single, closed view of spirituality, in the name of freedom and autonomy, albeit a form of paternalism which is benign.

Therefore it is necessary to accept the reality of a diversity of contrasting and conflicting spiritual traditions in contemporary culture. Wright goes on to address this issue by developing a generic definition of spirituality which attempts to affirm the quality of spirituality as common to humanity, whilst enabling each tradition to maintain its integrity.

> *'Spirituality is the developing relationship of the individual, within community and tradition, to that which is – or is perceived to be – of ultimate concern, ultimate value and ultimate truth' p 88*

It is this definition which facilitates an understanding of the whole child as a learner, with her own history, worldview and belief system and set of relationships within a tradition. It enables teachers to combine content and process, structure and direction, in the delivery of spiritual, moral, social and cultural development in the classroom. It facilitates an understanding of citizenship that maximises the importance of community, tradition and purpose, but without a universalising authoritarianism. It enables spiritual and moral formation to take place within the context of community, tradition and relationships in an open and appropriately critical context.

5. Learning & spiritual and moral development

Alongside the significant changes and opportunities in the provision of schooling and the emergence of a values agenda, there is another quiet revolution taking place which has Khunian significance as far as education and schooling is concerned. This has to do with the idea of learning and intelligence. Throughout modernity intelligence has been viewed as unitary, inborn, neural and a process – rather like a processor in a computer. However, increasingly this perception of intelligence is being challenged – by the idea of multiple intelligences, learnable intelligence, and the idea that knowledge, attitudes, experience and values are also highly pertinent to the notion of intelligence and learning. Clarke (Clark 1997) argues that intelligence/thinking/learning is a single, dynamic, mutli-faceted capacity...inherent in human consciousness and expressed in a variety of modes'.

Perhaps one of the most significant features of the current debates about spiritual and moral development is the assumption that it is something that is distinct from, and takes place separately from learning itself. Claxton (Claxton 1999) identifies some of the general assumptions about learning which Western culture tends to make. These are that 'learning is the acquisition of knowledge', that 'knowledge is true', that 'learning is for the young', that it involves teaching, that it 'proceeds calmly', that it is simple and that it 'involves understanding'. He goes on to present evidence that none of these assumptions stand up to scrutiny. He argues that learning involves self-knowledge, that learning power develops through culture, that it is multifarious and that it is not always fast or smooth. Some of the intrinsic components of learning include knowledge, know how, discriminations, preferences, dispositions, character and emotions.

Perkins (Perkins 1995) claims that we are at the beginning of a Copernican revolution concerning the nature of intelligence. He argues that, rather than being a fixed entity, intelligence is multi-dimensional, with three broad dimensions that are a) neural, b)experiential and c) reflective. Taken together these provide a new conception of intelligence that does not negate previous efforts to understand intelligent behaviour but incorporates them into a more dynamic, flexible and learnable quality. He suggests that the quality of reflective intelligence includes such components as metacognition and thinking skills, and also elements such as dispositions, concepts, beliefs and values. These dispositions, concepts, beliefs and values are acquired by persons-in-relation, who are located in communities, who have personal and social histories and who are participants in traditios. There is increasing evidence that a learner's worldview, values and beliefs are actually important learning tools, rather than things that have to be left outside the door of the learning institution.

Perkins (ibid) uses the metaphor of 'mirrors of mystery' to describe realms of thinking and learning i.e. they correspond directly with the kinds of mysteries, or things people do not know, which are encountered over and over again. These mysteries arise naturally as we strive to act effectively in the world; they reflect the nature of the world, and one mystery leads to another.

The notion of lifelong learning is relevant to this discussion. According to Smith and Spurling ([Smith, 1999 #94] lifelong learning relates to learning that takes place *throughout the lifespan*. It refers to learning with the widest possible boundaries, including the main types and classes of learning, and both informal and formal education and self-directed learning. It is relatively continuous, with a broad momentum that is maintained throughout life. It is intentional on the part of the individual or the organisation and is expressed in some form of personal or organisational strategy, formally or informally, which may be re-appraised over time.

At the moral level, lifelong learners are likely to live by four basic moral principles: personal commitment to learning; social commitment to learning; respect for others' learning and respect for truth. They argue that these principles have internal consistency even though they may be contested and are more difficult to verify empirically.

Smith and Spurling further argue that lifelong learning is linked conceptually with the values of democractic debate. These have to do with the value of group learning, in which the key dynamic is that individual members feel a sense of common purpose in the group, whilst at the same time feeling that the group recognises and values their individual contribution and potential. They cite Caine's [Cain, 1997 #207] biological learning theories which suggest that the brain seems to be programmed to learn in group situations, where security, personal individuation and group identity all work together to maximise the efficiency of learning.

It is clear that the notion of learning includes far more than merely cognitive development within a particular domain. Indeed the contemporary focus on learning to learn, and assessment for learning, rather than assessment of learning, brings together the two strands of personal and academic development into something approaching the formation of learners with community and tradition - and this is inseparable from that with individuals and communities hold to be of ultimate significance and value.

6. The conflict between lifeworld and systems world.

The substance of this paper has been concerned with the 'softer' side of schooling, with matters of values, beliefs and ultimate concerns as they influence schooling. It has been concerned with the 'culture' of schools, the 'normative glue' which hold things together. Sergiovanni (Sergiovanni 2000) describes this as 'the lifeworld of schools', drawing upon the social philosophy of Habermas.

According to Habermas the lifeworld is concerned with the ways in which human beings make meaning, in community. This is in contrast to the systems world, which is shaped by strategic rationality, or a means-end approach to managing the social and natural world. Society can be conceived from the perspective of acting subjects as the 'lifeworld of a social group' and also from the perspective of someone not involved as merely a 'system of actions' in which actions attain a functional value in line with their contribution to the maintenance of the system (Habermas 1973). The problem for Habermas was that any social theory that collapsed one of these aspects within the other is flawed. He argues that the proper connection can be made only when 'one develops the system concept out of the lifeworld concept'(ibid).

He focuses on language use and introduces discourse as the medium for co-ordinating action. He develops a view of the subject as an actor who relates simultaneously to all three worlds, with ordinary language competence giving them the capacity to use the entire system of world relations and validity claims in a distinct fashion for the purpose of co-ordinating action. He welcomes much of the feminist critique of moral development in which 'dialogue replaces logical deduction as the mode of moral discovery' and the procedural heart of which is 'a process of communication to discuss the other's position and discern the chain of connections through which the consequences of action extend' (Gilligan 1982) p45. He interprets this on the basis of his communicative model as a different aspect of a single richer voice that combines the two models of moral development.

Habermas sees the loss of freedom and the loss of meaning entailed by modernisation in terms of systemic threats to the communicative infrastructure through which the process of symbolic reproduction occurs. He says

> *'this communicative infrastructure is threatened by two tendencies which are intertwined and mutually reinforcing; by systemically induced reification and cultural impoverishment' (Habermas 1976) p483.*

The condition of advanced capitalism, according to Habermas, involves differentiated structures of a rationalised lifeworld in which actions are increasingly co-ordinated by consensual agreement rather than by normative prescriptions. He argues that strategic rationality is increasingly organised around the media of money and power and thus can be increasingly uncoupled from the lifeworld context. Habermas talks of the 'colonisation of the lifeworld' by strategic rationality, mediated through money and power, which constitute the social pathologies of modernity. This happens when the systemic media of money and power begin to displace communicative sociation in core spheres of action within which three processes of symbolic reproduction takes place; cultural transmission, social integration and socialisation.

The notion of lifeworld (Lebensweld) is important in understanding how action theory is linked with rationalistic processes. It is constituted by the more or less diffuse and unproblematic background convictions which stores the interpretive work of preceding generations and acts as a conservative counterweight to the risk of disagreement which arises with day-to-day processes of reaching an understanding. The 'colonisation of the lifeworld' results, according to Habermas, in 'cultural impoverishment' or loss of meaning.

One of the big challenges for education is how to integrate the strategic and rational aspects of schooling, concerned with maintaining the system effectively and efficiently and the lifeworld of schooling, which is concerned with meaning, purpose, vision and values – the term often used to describe this is 'hermeneutical rationality'. According to Sergiovanni these two worlds are both necessary and have to be successfully balanced for schools to be effective. However one of these two will always be generative - either the lifeworld determines the systems world or the systems world determines the lifeworld.

In 'Self Management and Diversity: Limits and Possibilities' (Deakin Crick 1996) the substantive issues of the research project led to the conclusion that the potential for profound educational change in schools will only occur in the presence of a communal orientation towards a hermeneutical understanding of the vocation of the school. This hermeneutical understanding is a movement or process stimulated by the presence of emancipatory rationality, which is often driven within schools by those individuals and groups on the margins of the school culture, as well as those leading. Strategic rationality is a means of controlling the objectified processes and procedures of schools and can be harnessed in the service of the school's hermeneutical self-understanding, rather than as an end in itself.

APPENDIX A Values Consultation, Autumn 97

Value Cluster	Y7	Y8	Y9	Y10	Y11	Y12/13	Tchrs	TOTAL
FRIEND SHIP / KINDNESS Love, acceptance, generosity, understanding, thoughtful, unselfishness, empathy, helpful + sharing, compassion, cooperation, supportive, caring,	24	15	5	3		6	9	62
HONESTY TRUTH INTEGRITY	5	4	4	3		9	6	31
TRUST LOYALTY TRUSTWORT HINESS	7	8	5	4		7	7	38
RESPECT FOR SELF, OTHERS + ENVIRONME NT	7	2	3	4		7	7	30
FAIRNESS listening, understanding others points of view, non judgemental, equality, justice.	3	1	2	4		6	7	23
FORGIVENESS	1	2	2			2	2	9
FAITH FAITHFULNE SS		1				1	2	4
EDUCATION GROWTH DEVELOPME NT patience, perseverance, maturity	1	3	1	1		2	1	9
NO OF TEACHING GROUPS	7	5	7	3		8		30
NO OF TEACHER RESPONSES							11	11

Character Dispositions: humour (7) reliable (5) responsible (2) attentive (2) optimistice/cheerful/confident (6) independence (1) sincerity (1) decisiveness (1) self discipline (1)

APPENDIX B Personal Construct Analysis: Pupils and Teachers

Constructs relating to:	Ts	Comments	Ps	Comments
Christian faith/ school	8	generally related to mood/ethos; one related to school's historical negative connections with slavery; strong awareness that this is a Christian school.	34	important for self - 16 important for school - 12 negative at emergent pole - 1 countered by need for tolerance 5
Positive Interpersonal relationships	4	caring relationships between pupils and teachers	35	friends and teachers
Community, working together, teamwork	5	including parents, pupils and teachers	3	working together
curriculum	5	related to breadth - broad = good. One related to particular categories for the mind. No mention of content.	3	related to variety of subjects
Learning/achievement, excellence	14	key role of learning and achievement	65	relating to growth, trying your best, working hard etc.
Equality, tolerance, all pupils equal	7	emphasis on education meeting all pupils needs regardless of ability	17	particular references to freedom of belief
Caring for the evironment	11	usually the school - creating a positive environment.	26	usually the school
Concern for whole person/pupil	6	not just the academic, including moral and social development		
Moral Development		see above	25	knowing right from wrong, being taught values,
Self identity -			29	individual expression, freedom. Standing up for oneself, following new ideas

APPENDIX C

School	Definitions for Pupils
Valuing Ourselves	Treating myself with respect; valuing my own feelings; knowing what I like and dislike; knowing what I think and feel; taking care of myself; taking care of my body; knowing what I want to do when I leave school; knowing how I learn; being committed to learning.
Valuing Others	Respecting other people; valuing other people's differences; taking care of other people; valuing our family, friends and communities.
Trustworthiness	Being trusted by others; doing what you say you will do; keeping promises; being a good friend.
Forgiveness	Being sorry and putting it right; letting go of being angry with someone when you have been wronged; starting over afresh.
Justice	Being fair; understanding and respecting the rules; treating all people and groups equally; taking care of people and groups who are disadvantaged.
Stewardship	Taking care of the environment; managing money carefully; conservation; taking careful responsibility for all my talents; gifts and belongings.
Truth	Telling the truth; trying to find out what is really true; knowing how to think about complex issues; keeping an open mind; listening to other people's ideas.
Fulfilling our potential	Finding out what my gifts and talents are; doing my best in everything; setting myself learning targets; planning what I want to do when I leave school; learning how I learn.
Faith in Christ	Having a faith of my own, or knowing why I don't; Knowing about the Christian faith; learning from the Christian faith;; understanding who Christ was and what the Christian story means for human society in 21C.

Bibliography

Barber, M. 1996 *The Learning Game: Arguments for an Education Revolution,,* London,: Victor Gollanz.

Barth, R. 1990 *Improving Schools from Within: Teachers, Parents and Principals Can Make a Difference,* San Francisco: Jossey Bass.

Beaudoin, T. 1998 *Virtual Faith The Irreverent Spirituality of Generation X,* San Francisco: Jossey-Bass.

Born P, Paula M, Mulligan J. & Price E 2002 *Ethics and Citizenship: Tools for Moral Decision Making,*London Hodder and Stoughton Educational

Bottery, M. 1990 *The Morality of the School*: London, Cassell Educational Ltd.

Chadwick, P. 1997 *Shifting Alliances Church & State in English Education,* London: Cassell.

Clark, E. 1997 *Designing and Implementing an Integrated Curriculum,* Brandon VT: Holistic Education Press.

Claxton, G. 1999 *Wise Up: The Challenge of Lifelong Learning,,* London: Bloomsbury.

Deakin Crick, R. 1996 'The Grant Maintained Status Policy: Self Management and Diversity: Limits and Possiblities' *Graduate School of Education,* Bristol: University of Bristol.

Deakin Crick, R. e. a. 2000 *Achieving a Whole School Approach to the Spiritual, Moral, Social and Cultural Development of Pupils,,* Bristol: EducareM.

Delaney, C. 1994 *The Liberalism-Communitarianism Debate*: London, Rowman & Littlefield Publishers,Inc.

Department, f., Education,, 1992 *Choice and Diversity, A New Framework for Schools*: London, HMSO.

DFEE 2000 *The National Curriculum Handbook for teachers in England,* London: The Stationary Office.

Ernest, P. 1991 *The Philosophy of Mathematics*: Basingstoke, The Falmer Press.

Feyerabend, P. 1975 *Against Method*: London, Verso.

Fullan, M. 1993 *Change Forces: Probing the Depths of Educational Reform*: London, The Falmer Press.

— 1999 *Change forces : the sequel,* Philadelphia, Pa.: Falmer Press.

Gilligan, C. 1982 *In a Different Voice: Psychological Theory and Women's Development*: Cambridge MA, Harvard University Press.

Habermas, J. 1973 'Knowledge and Human Interests': Cambridge, Polity.

— 1976 'Communication and the Evolution of Society,': Cambridge, Polity.

Halstead, J. T., M. 2000 *The Development ofValues, Attitudes and Personal Qualities A Review of Recent Research,*, Slough,: National Foundation for Educational Research.

Harman, W. 1988 *Global Mind Change*, Indianapolis: Knowledge Systems.

Hirst, P. 1974 *Knowledge and the Curriculum,*: London, Routledge /Kegan Paul.

Hull, J. (ed) 1996 *The Ambiguity of Spiritual Values*: London, The Falmer Press.

Kegan, R. 1994 *In Over Our Heads: The Mental Demands of Modern Life,*, Cambridge MA.: Harvard University Press.

Kidder, R. 1994 *Shared Values for a Troubled World*, San Francisco: Jossey Bass.

Kuhn, T. 1970 *2nd Edn The Structure of Scientific Revolutions*: Chicago University of Chicago Press.

Lakatos, I. 1978 *Mathematics, Science and Epistemology,*: Cambridge, Cambridge University Press.

MacIntyre, A. 1992 *The Virtues, the Unity of Human Life and the Concept of a Tradition, in Sandel M.(ed) Liberalism and its Critics,*: Oxford, Backwell Publishers.

Marsh, J. 1993 *The Strategic Toolkit,*: Bedford, IFS International Ltd.

Moody, T. (ed) 1994 *Some Comparisons Between Liberalism and an Eccentric Communitarianism*: London, Rowman /Littlefield Pub.Inc.

NCC 1993 *Spiritual and Moral Development: A Discussion Paper*, York: National Curriculum Council.

OFSTED 2000 *Inspecting Schools The Framework*, London: OFSTED.

Perkins, D. 1995 *Outsmarting IQ: The emerging Science of Learnable Intelligence,*, New York,: Free Press.

Polanyi, M. 1958 *Personal Knowledge: Towards a Post Critical Philosophy,*: London, Routledge /Kegan Paul.

Popper, K. (ed) 1970 *Normal Science and its Dangers*: Cambridge,Cambridge University Press.

Postman, N. 1996 *The End of Education*, New York: Vintage Books.

Rawls, J. 1971 *A Theory of Justice,*: Cambridge Mass., Harvard University Press.

Rogers, C. and Stevens. 1973 *Person to Person: The Problem of Being Human A New Trend in Psychology,*: London, Souvenir Press.

Sacks, J. 2000 'The Judaic Vision of Citizenship Education', in N. H. J. Pearce (ed) *Tomorrow's Citizens Critical Debates in Citizenship and Education*, London: IPPR.

Sandel, M. 1984 *Liberalism and its Critics,*: Oxford, Backwell Publishers.

Sergiovanni, T. 2000 *The Lifeworld of Leadership Creating Culture, Community and Personal Meaning in our Schools,*, San Francisco: Jossey Bass.

Shortt, J. F., A. (ed) 1996 *The Charis Project*, Nottingham: The Stapleford Centre.

Sunderland, C., Deakin Crick, R., Peskelt, D. 2001 *A Conceptual Framework for Citizenship Education.* University of Bristol Graduate School of Education, Bristol.

Talbot, M. T., N. 1997 'Shared Values in a Pluralist Society?', in R. S. P. Smith (ed) *Teaching Right and Wrong Moral Education in the Balance*, London: Trentham Books Ltd.

Tate, N. 2000 'Citizenship education in a liberal democracy', in N. H. J. Pearce (ed) *Tomorrows Citizens Critical Debates in Citizenship and Education*, London: IPPR.

Taylor, C. 1984 *Hegel: History and Politics, in Sandel M.(ed) Liberalism and its Critics,*: Oxford, Blackwell.

Tillich, P. 1959 *Theology of Culture*, New York: Oxford University Press.

Walford, G. 1995 'The Northbourne Amendments: is the House of Lords a Garbage Can?', *Journal of Education Policy* 10(4).

White, S. 1988 *The Recent Work of Jurgen Habermas,*: Cambridge, Cambridge University Press.

Wright, A. 1998 *Spiritual Pedagogy A Survey, Critique and Reconstruction of Contemporary Spiritual Education in England and Wales*, Abingdon: Cullham College Institute.